GW01375327

*Forerunners
of the
All Blacks*

Forerunners of the All Blacks

The 1888-89 New Zealand Native Football Team in Britain, Australia and New Zealand

Greg Ryan

Canterbury University Press

Publication of this book has been assisted by the
Historical Branch of the Department of Internal Affairs

First published in 1993 by
CANTERBURY UNIVERSITY PRESS
University of Canterbury, Private bag 4800,
Christchurch, New Zealand

Copyright © 1993 Greg Ryan
Copyright © 1993 Canterbury University Press

ISBN 0-908812-30-2 (casebound)
ISBN 0-908812-35-3 (Collectors' Limited Edition)

This book is copyright. Except for the purpose of fair review, no part may be stored or transmitted in any form or by any means, electronic or mechanical, including recording or storage in any information retrieval system, without permission in writing from the publisher. No reproduction may be made, whether by photocopying or any other means, unless a licence has been obtained from the publisher or its agent.

Designed and typeset by Hazard Publication Services
Jacket design by Richard King/Edsetera
Jacket photo of the author by Monique Ford
Printed through Bookprint Consultants,
Wellington

Contents

List of illustrations 6
Acknowledgements 7
Introduction 9
1   A sporting endeavour? 11
2   A winning formula 22
3   The honour of the colony 31
4   "Maori enough" 43
5   Players, profits and promoters 57
6   Exploits and exploitation 67
7   Gentlemen and competitors 80
8   "Quiet and well behaved"? 96
9   "Playing stiff" 107
10 Much more than a circus 114
Conclusion 124
Notes 128
Appendix 1: The players 133
               The management 140
Appendix 2: Match record 141
Appendix 3: Individual records 145
Bibliographical note 149
Index 151

Illustrations

Joe Warbrick	13
Formal team photo of the 1888 British touring team.	16
Sketch of the 1888 British touring team.	20
The 1884 New Zealand team to Australia	22
The five Warbrick brothers	24
Tabby Wynyard	26
Patrick Keogh	29
The Native team cap	31
New Zealand Native team	35
Native team "play up" card	44
The Surrey team cheering the 'Maories' on their appearance	45
Charles Goldsmith scoring the first goal for the Native team	48
The press play on British imagination	53
The first haka by a New Zealand rugby team in Britain	54
New Zealand Native team. Possibly before the Middlesex match	60
David Gage	65
Native team season tickets	67
The 1889 Ireland team which defeated Wales	72
Three cheers at the conclusion of the Surrey match	76
George Williams	79
Andrew Stoddart	84
The 1889 England team	87
Rowland Hill	90
Punch magazine's comment on rough play	92
Two umpires, Joe Warbrick and a Surrey official	94
"A sudden outburst of joy on getting the 1st goal of the tour"	97
The team card from the match against Oxford University	98
Caricatures of the Reverend Frank Marshall and James Miller	101
Tom Ellison	106
Members of the Native team in Queensland	109
Charles Speakman	112
Billy Warbrick	112
Patrick Keogh	117
The 1892 Wellington representative team	119
A Warbrick family group	122

Acknowledgements

The debts I have accumulated over the last three years relate mainly to my MA thesis from which this book is derived.

I am particularly grateful to Jock Phillips and the Historical Branch, Department of Internal Affairs, for a research bursary which enabled me to travel to Britain for work in the Colindale newspaper library.

For their help in obtaining hundreds of newspaper volumes, not all readily accessible, I owe much to the staff of the University of Canterbury Library, Canterbury Public Library, Hocken Library, Dunedin, National Library and Parliamentary Library, Wellington, and especially the British Library Newspaper Library, Colindale, London. Many of the photographs were kindly provided by the New Zealand Rugby Museum, Palmerston North. Thanks also to Ron Palenski, Russell Vine and Timothy Auty for their assistance in this area.

My greatest debts are personal. My family have provided constant encouragement and practical assistance in London and Palmerston North. In Christchurch this project was sustained by the advice and friendship of Sue Cook, Brent Giblin, Liz Parker, Nic Wright and Annelies Krijgsman, among others.

Rod Chester responded to a multitude of obscure questions and supplied me with much material from his own considerable research into New Zealand rugby.

Luke Trainor, Chris Connolly and Vincent Orange of the History Department, University of Canterbury, provided valuable ideas and references.

During the transformation from thesis to book, Mike Bradstock of Canterbury University Press gave numerous useful hints and directions, as did John Small.

Two people in particular have been of invaluable help. Barbara Chinn has always understood the complex life of a thesis writer and computer user and may one day find an outlet for her newly acquired knowledge of nineteenth-century sport. Above all, I wish to thank Len Richardson who first alerted me to the research potential of the Native tour, supervised my thesis, oversaw this transformation of it and has always given me the confidence to develop my ideas.

Introduction

Which was the greatest New Zealand rugby touring team? This question is often asked but it can never be satisfactorily answered. It is almost impossible to compare individuals and teams from different periods or to judge the relative strength of their opponents. Statistical comparisons can be equally unrewarding because other factors must be considered with them. What follows therefore is not an attempt to answer the question definitively, although some judgements are offered. Rather, this book seeks to bring to light the record of one team whose pioneering achievements have been largely forgotten.

When the New Zealand Native Football Representatives returned home from Britain and Australia in August 1889 they were regarded as a great team. Their brand of sensational running rugby and combined forward play had never been seen before in New Zealand. In their touring record they were not "invincible" in the sense that the 1924 All Blacks deserved that accolade. But in a fourteen-month, 107-match marathon they had defeated Ireland, held Wales to a narrow margin and downed most of the strongest county and club sides in England. They gave a model of skill to guide New Zealand rugby into the future.

It was seventeen years before another New Zealand team followed in these pioneering footsteps. This next team, dubbed "The Originals", played less than a third of the matches of their predecessors, and yet they returned home to a permanent place in the national consciousness. The Native team, however, gradually slipped into anecdotal obscurity. This account aims to rescue it by tracing its origins, assessing the motives and methods of its promoters, examining its achievements and considering the character of its players.

In some respects it is not surprising that the New Zealand public forgot the Native team. The main account of the tour was written by its promoter, Thomas Eyton, but nothing substantial from the players has survived. Newspaper sources give a patchwork of detail, but at every turn there are gaps and sometimes crucial omissions.

In another sense the forgetting of the tour might have been deliberate. Although they were hailed as great players, the Native team were also charged with behaviour which rugby administrators have always tried to stamp out — professionalism, unsporting conduct, drunkenness. No one would call them angelic. But it is equally clear that many of the features of the tour which led to their fall from grace were part and parcel of the nineteenth-century sporting ethos. There were allies aplenty for the team, but not for the last time there was a tinge of hypocrisy in the attitude of rugby officialdom.

The timing of the tour was also crucial. Within seven years of its conclusion, British rugby split between the conservative forces of gentlemanly amateurism, represented by the Rugby Football Union, and the working-class pragmatism of the Northern Rugby Football Union which later became changed to Rugby Football League. Throughout their time in Britain the Native team trod a difficult line between the two distinctly emerging camps and the contrasting class values they embraced. Frequently the team found themselves among the rebels and for that they paid the consequences.

This book is much more than the chronology of a rugby tour. The Native team were predominantly Maori in a place and time where such foreigners were a great rarity, and they were the subject of intense curiosity. They were also colonists under the scrutiny of an imperial elite to whom sport was much more than a game. And whatever the team did, there were many in New Zealand who felt that their actions could make or break the wider reputation of the young colony.

What binds these themes together is the story of twenty-six players who suffered illness, injury and frequently unscrupulous treatment, and yet still were able to achieve an outstanding playing record on the longest tour in rugby history.

1
A sporting endeavour?

New Zealand's 17-11 victory over England at Twickenham on 3 January 1925 marked both a high and low point for "The Invincibles". It set this remarkable team apart as the first international rugby tourists ever to go through Britain without losing or drawing a game. But in the early minutes of that match Cyril Brownlie became the first All Black to be sent off in a test when referee Albert Freethy dismissed him for allegedly over-zealous mauling. Thankfully for Brownlie, there were no serious repercussions from his hosts, the Rugby Football Union. He was regarded as unfortunate to be in the wrong place at the wrong time. The incident was not allowed to detract from the achievements of an All Black team which won thirty-two matches in succession, scored 838 points to 116 and propelled one of its Maori players, George Nepia, to something approaching stardom.

Brownlie's fate might have had a special significance for one elderly Rugby Football Union official who was at that match. Almost thirty-six years earlier, on a wet and bitterly cold afternoon in February 1889, George Rowland Hill had had his own acrimonious encounter with a New Zealand team. As both Union secretary and international referee, Hill had awarded not one but three hotly disputed England tries against a battered and weary New Zealand Native team in the fifty-fourth match of their British tour. One try in particular infuriated the visitors. It was scored while the majority of them claimed to be forming a protective circle around the England player, Andrew Stoddart, who had ripped his shorts in a tackle.

The reaction of the Native team was not merely to argue with Hill's decisions, a disturbing enough response to a sporting gentleman, but for three of them to walk off the field in disgust. Only heated negotiation between team management and senior players persuaded the three to return and take their place in a comprehensive and controversial defeat by England.

But the matter did not rest. The Rugby Football Union immediately demanded a formal apology, threatening to cancel the remainder of the tour. When the apology arrived it was deemed unsatisfactory and Hill dictated another to be signed by the match captain Mac McCausland. Six weeks later, when the Native team returned to London for their final match in Britain, few leading players could be found to oppose them and the officials of the Union did not offer a farewell. It was seventeen years before another New Zealand team returned to the home of rugby.

And the legacy persists. There is not a single account of the New Zealand Native team which does not dwell on the England international and the controversy that went with it, or on the off-field behaviour of some team members. The tour has assumed a place in New Zealand rugby history as something of a circus. It is regarded as best left in the past — a long way behind the more respectable and supposedly more formidable achievements of the 1905 and 1924 All Blacks.

Yet if we look beyond the popular myth, beyond the hypocrisy of Rowland Hill and his colleagues, we see a team whose playing record is possibly superior to that of their much-eulogized successors. Off the field they were welcomed and respected in most quarters. Many understood and supported their grievances against Rugby Football Union authority and saw conflict as inevitable. And by the time they returned to New Zealand the Native team had fine-tuned their skills and innovations into a style that would transform New Zealand rugby from nineteenth-century folk football to a twentieth-century national game.

The Native tour entailed far more than merely the selection of a team, the arrangement of an itinerary and the playing of matches. To understand the full story, one needs to know something about the state of New Zealand rugby during the 1880s, and especially Maori rugby, but more particularly about the motives of those who organized and financed the Native team. These motives, far more than the ability of the players, shaped everything during the long tour. When plans for a privately organized tour of Britain and Australia were first announced in the summer of 1888, reaction was anything but light-hearted. The New Zealand provincial rugby unions saw the team as a possible threat to their control of the game. The mysterious blend of sport and financial speculation involved in the tour did not sit comfortably with the gentlemanly view that sport should be played for pleasure and not profit. When the Maori team went "home" to Britain, there was ample reason to wonder whether they would convey a favourable picture of New Zealand rugby, and of the colony in general. Nor did it help that there was to be a mixture of Maori and Pakeha players at a time when the future of relationships between the two peoples was uncertain. At the centre of the debate which was about to unfold stood one man — Joseph Astbury Warbrick.

Warbrick was unquestionably the founding father of the Native team. Born at Rotorua in 1862 to a Maori mother and Pakeha father, he attended St Stephen's Native School until 1877, the same year in which he made his provincial rugby debut as Auckland full-back at the age of only fifteen. As a Government servant he travelled widely throughout the North Island, representing Wellington during the 1879 and 1880 seasons before reappearing for Auckland in 1882 and 1883. The

A sporting endeavour?

Joe Warbrick as he appeared for the New Zealand team to Australia in 1884. Rugby Museum, Palmerston North

following year, along with Jack Taiaroa of Otago, Warbrick became one of the first Maori players to represent New Zealand on the pioneering tour to Australia. There he distinguished himself by landing three dropped goals in his seven appearances which included the three main fixtures of the tour against New South Wales.

Back in New Zealand, Warbrick represented Hawke's Bay in 1885, Auckland in 1886 and Hawke's Bay again in 1887. As either a full-back or three-quarter he won considerable praise for his speed, ball skills and drop-kicking. His abilities were matched by few in the colony, and among Maori players only by Taiaroa. S.E. Sleigh, manager of the 1884 New Zealand team to Australia, described him as "a player without a vestige of funk; he will dash at an opponent at full speed and collar him, very fast and an untiring individual".[1]

At the beginning of 1888 Warbrick was apparently still living in Hawke's Bay. It has been assumed that his inspiration to organize the Native team came from R.L. Seddon's British football team which first visited New Zealand in April 1888. Warbrick, making a guest appearance for the Wellington team on 14 May, is said to have taken much heart from their 3-all draw with the tourists and immediately set about assembling a team for Britain.

However, it is quite clear that his actions were far more than a sudden impulse. Plans had been made long before the Wellington match; indeed, long before the British team had even arrived in New Zealand. In a letter circulated to the press in early February 1888, Warbrick announced his intention to select a team of Maori or part-Maori players to play the British when they arrived in April. He also held no doubts about the success of such a team:

> [I] am anxious to select the very best men I can ... We will be able to muster a really first class team, and I feel convinced we could render a good account of ourselves ... I am not sure of the balance, but anticipate that when complete they would be good enough for anything in New Zealand.[2]

Players in Wairarapa and Taranaki had already been contacted, Jack Taiaroa was trying to interest his brother Dick, his cousin Tom Ellison, and another Wellington player, David Gage. Warbrick himself was contacting the Wynyard brothers of Auckland and other players in the Thames district. He hoped that the match would be played at Auckland where gate takings would be likely to cover the high costs.

By early March this Auckland match had evolved into far grander plans. In an interview given while he was passing through Christchurch in search of suitable players, Warbrick announced that his team would play the British only if he could arrange a suitable division of gate money to cover his costs. Furthermore, although he had abandoned plans to take a team to Sydney, he indicated that he would take one to Britain if a preliminary tour of New Zealand proved successful. A month later it was reported that the Rugby Football Union in England had been working hard to foster interest in the tour since it had first been suggested to them by S.E. Sleigh in October 1887. In fact the Union extended its patronage to the tour by early April 1888, just before the British team arrived in New Zealand. Warbrick later claimed that for several years he had been pressed to form a team "that would do for Maori football what the Australians have done for Australian cricket and make it famous", although he never revealed who had "pressed" him to do this.[3] It is certain, then, that Warbrick did not need the British team as his guiding light.

Quite coincidentally, at the same time as Warbrick was revealing his plans in New Zealand, similar ideas were emerging from another source — Thomas Eyton. Born in Essex in 1843, Eyton came to New Zealand in 1862 and served for seven years with the Taranaki Bushrangers and the Patea Light Horse in the Anglo-Maori wars. He then served for two years with the Armed Constabulary in Wanganui before moving to Wellington to take a job in Treasury. His rugby experience consisted mainly of appearances for the Armed Constabulary and for Civil Service teams in Wellington during the early 1870s.[4]

However, in 1887, while in England for Queen Victoria's Jubilee year, Eyton witnessed a number of important rugby matches — especially at the Rectory Field, Blackheath, where England often played home internationals in the days before Twickenham was established. In his book about the Native team's tour, *Rugby Football Past and Present*, he later wrote:

A sporting endeavour?

It seemed to me that the play I saw was not vastly superior to that I had seen in New Zealand and that if a team from this colony — especially Maoris or half-castes — could be taken to England and brought to up-to-date form, such a venture would prove a success in every respect.[5]

How or when Warbrick and Eyton became aware of each other's plans is not known. Nor is it certain whether Sleigh was representing only one or both of them when he approached the Rugby Football Union in 1887. Eyton's only recollection was that after hearing of Warbrick's plans he immediately contacted him, and after a period of doubt about securing the necessary players and finance, it was decided to proceed with the tour. At some time during April or May 1888, James Scott, a publican from Gisborne, was also added to the partnership, although his connection with the other two is again unknown. It was decided that Warbrick would act as team captain, Scott as manager and Eyton as promoter and treasurer.

Without the example of the British team playing in New Zealand, a private tour to Britain would seem a considerable undertaking only eighteen years after the first game of rugby had been played in New Zealand. Indeed, rugby as a whole was a very young game. Although "folk football" had been played in British villages and schools for centuries, there were no standard rules, team sizes or playing fields. Games involving hundreds of players could roam for hours through streets and across parish boundaries leaving a trail of destruction and sometimes death. Not until the old boys of public schools brought their various football codes to the universities of Oxford and Cambridge during the 1840s, was some attempt made to standardize rules. If these men were to play against each other, they needed common understandings.

Finding the best formula was not made any easier by the pride and stubbornness of many of those involved. The old public schools such as Eton and Harrow refused to be dictated to by others, and clung determinedly to a kicking game. Newer schools, such as Rugby, were equally set on making a name for themselves by promoting a handling game. Although a "Cambridge compromise", which allowed both, was played during the 1850s, this was not altogether satisfactory. Finally, a meeting called in London in 1863 established a single code. The result was the formation of the Football Association, which agreed on a kicking game which became known as soccer. Rugby School and its supporters still refused to abandon the handling game.

For a time compromise seemed possible when the Football Association suggested that it might be prepared to tolerate some handling. But a permanent rift was assured by a strong clash of opinion over the issue of "hacking" — the deliberate kicking of an opponent's shins. The secretary of the Football Association declared that, "If we have hacking, no one who has arrived at the age of discretion will play at football and it will be entirely left to schoolboys."

An official of the Blackheath Club replied that hacking was "the true form of football; if you do away with it, you will do away with all of the courage and pluck of the game, and I will be bound to bring over a lot of Frenchmen who would beat you with a week's practice". So in 1871 Rugby School and other supporters of the handling and hacking game went their own way and formed the Rugby Football Union. Ironically, one of its first legislative moves was to outlaw hacking. Like the Football Association, they quickly realized that if sport was to be played by men in business, it had to be safe.[6]

Rugby spread quickly to New Zealand as public school old boys arrived in the colony. The first encounter was between Town and School at Nelson in 1870. Clubs were soon formed in all of the main centres, and even in small country towns such as Temuka and Rangitikei by the middle of the decade. Beginning with Canterbury and Wellington in 1879, twelve provincial rugby unions had been founded by 1888 and two more were to follow in 1890. Auckland undertook the first provincial tour in 1875, and New South Wales, the first rugby team to tour overseas, visited New Zealand in 1882 and again in 1886. New Zealand returned the visit in 1884. Thus when the British team arrived in 1888 rugby was well established and growing. But as an international sport it still had nothing like the touring record of cricket.

Given such rapid growth, it is easy enough to understand Joe Warbrick organizing a Native team based on purely sporting objectives. By the 1880s Maori were making their own distinct contribution to New Zealand rugby. Exclusively Maori clubs

The 1888 British touring team. Although not the inspiration for the Native team, the British boosted New Zealand rugby with many new techniques, especially in back play. Rugby Museum, Palmerston North

were formed, such as the Hauraki club at Kiri Kiri, near Thames, in 1883, but most players were content to merge with Pakeha teams. Maori names can be found in teams throughout the 1870s: Wirihana appeared in a twenty-a-side match at Aramaho on 22 June 1872, Takeru was in the Rangitikei side of 1876, and in the Otago High School Rectory team of 1878 there were two Taiaroa brothers, one of whom joined Warbrick in the first New Zealand team.

Like early Pakeha rugby, much Maori rugby can be traced to secondary schools. St Stephen's Native School and Te Aute College encouraged a high standard of play from the early 1880s, Te Aute, especially, imparting many of the athletic values of English public schools during the headmastership of John Thornton (1878-1910). Indeed, one pupil at the college defended rugby against accusations of roughness by informing his critic that it was "essential and natural for the young to indulge in some wholesome form of sport".[7] It is equally likely that many of the smaller Native Schools strongly encouraged their pupils to play rugby or various forms of "folk" football which still remained popular during the 1870s.

It is not surprising then, that of the twenty-one Maori players who left New Zealand with the Native team, six came from Te Aute College, one had been at Christchurch Boys High School, and Joe Warbrick had attended St Stephen's. His four brothers and the three Wynyard brothers in the team may also have been influenced in their rugby by attending various well established schools in Auckland and Tauranga.

With the strong school network, and his own diverse experiences in provincial rugby, Warbrick was in a better position than anyone to assess Maori talent and prospects for a tour. It is quite plausible that, having played for New Zealand in 1884, he was captivated by the idea of taking a team representing the Maori people on a tour to the home of rugby. Warbrick was also quite aware of the potential of touring sports teams. His desire to put Maori rugby on a level akin to Australian cricket acknowledged a pattern dating back to the 1860s. An English cricket team was in Australia for some part of every year from 1881 to 1888, and this gesture was reciprocated at two-yearly intervals from 1878, the Australian "Ashes" victory at Lords in 1882 being an especially notable achievement.

Whether Warbrick had any reason to expect success for his team is another matter. No Maori players had the experience of British rugby to make any useful comparisons, and no representative Maori team of any description had been selected before 1888. Aside from unofficial combinations which took the field against Great Britain in 1904 and Australia in 1905, there was not to be one until 1910. In fact, of the Maori players Warbrick chose for either the proposed Auckland match or the final Native team, only eight had any previous experience of provincial rugby.

Eyton's account of the Native tour reveals that sport was not the only objective: money loomed large in his calculations. He claimed that the tour had to be a private venture because the New Zealand provincial unions insisted that no team should travel overseas except under their management. Having guaranteed £2000 for the tour, he and James Scott felt entitled to have a major control over the management and selection of the team. Indeed, the administrative structure of the game during the 1880s undoubtedly lent itself to such private arrangements. Until the New Zealand Rugby Football Union was formed in 1892, there was often inefficiency and even acrimony among the provincial bodies. This presented opportunities to make arrangements outside "establishment" boundaries.

Nevertheless, Eyton's criticism of the provincial unions is rather tenuous. The unions agreed to play matches against the Native team before its departure from New Zealand, and to share gate receipts from these matches with the tour promoters. Hence they at least tolerated the tour. The only real point of controversy arose when Pakeha players were added to what was originally a Maori team. By that time the unions had already supported it in three matches, and they did not withdraw their patronage after this controversy.

Eyton depicted the unions as hostile because he wanted to make money out of the tour at a time when the conservative supporters of amateurism were fighting to keep their hold on rugby. He presented himself to the public not as a financial speculator, but as an innovator battling against an obstructive and fragmented establishment. Yet his true position is displayed in his failure to explain why he wanted an exclusively Maori team. Warbrick had a much greater knowledge of Maori playing strength, and Eyton in fact played no part in the selection of the team. He did not even meet them, or Warbrick, until the party reached Christchurch for its sixth match against Canterbury on 21 July. Relying entirely on Maori players seems to rule out any notion of Eyton wanting to assemble a fully representative team to enhance the reputation of New Zealand rugby and the colony as a whole in Britain.

Certainly Eyton's plan was partly an appeal to ordinary rugby followers. This was after all to be the first international rugby team to tour Britain. But to conduct the tour using only Maori players strongly suggests that it was aimed at a much wider section of the British public. The British were fascinated with indigenous representatives of the colonies during the nineteenth century, and there were handsome profits to be made from their visits. Numerous promoters filled their pockets by parading Maori, Aborigine and African visitors before a paying public who had seldom, if ever, seen non-white people.

A direct parallel with Eyton's objective for the Native tour was the visit of an Aboriginal cricket team to England in 1868. Organised and captained by Charles Lawrence, a member of the first English team to visit Australia in 1861-2, the team won fourteen and lost fourteen of its forty-seven matches on a five-month tour. If their cricket was not always up to standard, the Aborigines quickly won a following for their appearance, athletic prowess and traditional weapons displays. They regularly won throwing competitions and races against professional sprinters. One of the team, named Dick-a-Dick, using only a club and a thin shield, constantly amazed spectators by fending from his body a number of cricket balls thrown simultaneously and forcefully. The gate receipts from these exhibitions helped to give the promoters of the tour a profit of over £1400.

Whether or not Eyton knew about this tour, it is a safe assumption that during his visit to Britain in 1887 he investigated the response to previous Maori visitors and the likely reception for a touring football team. And he was certainly not alone in recognizing its financial potential. For as soon as the tour became public knowledge in New Zealand, there was a scramble between a number of parties who recognized the opportunity for easy profits.

Early in May 1888 Warbrick announced that there would be no problem securing preliminary finance to get the team to Britain. One gentleman, probably Eyton, had offered him £2000, and £3000 could have been secured in Auckland alone. Another with a strong desire to become involved was a Mr Brown, a Scotsman from Christchurch. According to two letters by Arthur Shrewsbury, the noted English test cricketer and promoter of the 1888 British football team, Brown met Warbrick early in May and offered to put £400 into the venture provided that certain conditions were met — although it is not known what these were. According to Brown, members of the team were not satisfied with Warbrick's arrangements for the tour. He therefore attempted to strengthen his case by suggesting that he would entice these players to join with the promoters of the British team who were apparently planning to organize their own New Zealand team to tour Britain. Finally, when Warbrick still refused his offer, and the British plan failed to materialize, Brown, rather ironically, joined the camp of those who criticized the Native team for being professionals.[8]

When Warbrick visited the Wairarapa in search of players at the beginning of March 1888, profits rather than rugby were uppermost in many minds. While a number of local Maori were keen to play the British in a match at Auckland, they were not enthusiastic about a full tour. They were sceptical about Warbrick's inclusion of part-Maori players, feeling that only full-blooded Maori, who looked the part, would be an effective drawcard and source of profit in Britain.[9] This concern was obviously not with playing strength. A team of full-blooded Maori would have had even less justification in rugby terms than that already proposed by Warbrick. As it transpired, of the full-blooded Maori players in the Native team, only Rene and Taiaroa had any previous experience of provincial rugby. The concern voiced most loudly in the Wairarapa was more

The 1888 British team. This sketch was done on board ship shortly before the team reached New Zealand. Russell Vine

evidently that if the team did not present the appearance and character of true Maori, they would not attract the interest of the British public.

Motives for the tour were also raised in parliament by William Pember Reeves, himself a noted sporting identity who had played rugby and cricket for Canterbury. In a question to Thomas Fergus, the Minister of Public Works, asking whether the Native team was to be given free rail travel while in New Zealand, Reeves declared that it was widely understood that the tour was merely a speculation and that the team was neither truly native nor representative.[10]

The best evidence for Eyton and Scott's financial objective comes from what happened during the tour itself. In Eyton's *Rugby Football Past and Present*, and in Scott's frequent comments to the London correspondent of the *Lyttelton Times*, there are numerous references to financial matters. Problems such as fluctuating gate receipts, travel and accommodation expenses, and shortfalls caused by the free admission of spectators to some matches, all caused Eyton and Scott much greater worry than seems normal for sports promoters in search of a satisfactory break-even point.

To some extent making money was a necessity. Without initial capital, and regular income thereafter, Warbrick's grand plans could never have come to reality. The question is: how much was enough to ensure the security of the tour, and how much was enough to secure a handsome profit? It might be assumed that those who held the purse strings held sway. But Warbrick's claim that there were many willing speculators indicates that he held a flexible bargaining position — one in which he could have chosen financial backers on terms satisfactory to his own sporting objectives for the tour. Unfortunately a severe foot injury sustained in the third tour match against Auckland on 7 July restricted Warbrick's role as a player to only twenty-one of the 107 matches. Forced to direct his attention more towards management and other off-field matters, it seems that he too became concerned with profits and lost sight of the difficulties facing the rest of the team. As the toll of injuries and illnesses mounted and more games were added to the tour itinerary, serious divisions emerged between some of the players and the need or desire of the promoters to make money from them.

2
A winning formula

Warbrick's overriding concern during the early months of 1888 was to assemble the strongest possible team from the limited pool of Maori players. Unlike Charles Lawrence, who drew his Aboriginal cricket team from a small district of Western Victoria and included perhaps five genuine players in its fourteen members, Warbrick cast his net from Hokianga to Southland in search of talent. The contrast with Lawrence's lopsided selection policy shows that in cricket, far more than in rugby, a small number of skilled individuals can carry the performances of others. Pride also placed demands on a player of Warbrick's standing. If Maori people were to be presented before the British public, all steps should be taken to ensure that they were the best.

Even Eyton and Scott, who regarded rugby more as the excuse than the purpose for the tour, needed a team with potential to win most of their matches. If the Native team performed poorly and established a reputation as "easybeats", their ability to draw paying spectators through the turnstiles would rapidly

The 1884 New Zealand team to Australia, including Joe Warbrick and Jack Taiaroa. Rugby Museum, Palmerston North

diminish. While a group of Maori would always attract the curious gaze in British streets, a profit could be made only in the regulated environment of a sports ground where the public saw some reason to pay for their pleasure. Uninspiring and unsuccessful teams do not draw crowds.

How Warbrick assembled the Native team is not clear. Eyton played no part in the selection process, conducting all of his business with Warbrick and Scott by letter and not meeting them until the team reached Christchurch in July. But he does hint at some difficulties with player availability. Of the twenty-two players named by Warbrick in March for the proposed Auckland match against the British, only eleven made it to Britain. Of those who withdrew, five came from the Wairarapa where there had been opposition to Warbrick's inclusion of part-Maori players. Three other players who assembled with the Native team at Napier in April also failed to make the tour. By far the greatest loss from the original selection was Jack Taiaroa. A superb all-round athlete, he was the leading try scorer on the 1884 tour to Australia, later set a New Zealand long jump record at 20 feet 11 inches (6.39 metres) and played eight seasons of representative cricket for Hawke's Bay. But his valuable services were lost to the Native team due to university commitments.

If the team finally selected was somewhat weaker than intended, it still had strong credentials. The most striking feature was the inclusion of Joe Warbrick's four brothers — William, Alfred, Arthur and Fred. It is tempting to see these selections as convenient and not based strictly on merit. However, William (Billy) Warbrick, for one, was a player of proven ability. He gained selection for Bay of Plenty Combined Clubs in 1882 at the age of about sixteen and later appeared for Auckland in 1886 and 1890. Moving to Australia with his brother Fred, he represented Queensland twice against New Zealand in 1893, and New South Wales against them in 1897. A non-drinker and non-smoker, Billy Warbrick was a fearless, if injury-prone, full-back and an adventurous runner whom Eyton came to regard as the best player in the Native team.

Alf and Arthur Warbrick were regular players for the Matata club in the Bay of Plenty, the latter winning repute as much for his hard forward play as for a seventeen-inch calf measurement. The ability of the youngest brother, Fred, was evident in his fine performances for the Native team and his appearances for Queensland during the early 1890s.[1]

Close family and playing links point to the inclusion of several other team members. Jack Taiaroa was instrumental in persuading his younger brother, Dick, and his cousin, Tom Ellison, to join the team. The younger Taiaroa acquired his early rugby training at Christchurch Boys High School, represented Wellington in 1886 and 1887 and Hawke's Bay in 1889. Ellison was to emerge as one of the outstanding figures of New Zealand rugby. After a distinguished

The five Warbrick brothers, photographed during the early 1890s. Three were to die as the result of accidents in the years 1902-4. Rugby Museum, Palmerston North

career at Te Aute College, he was a regular member of the Wellington team from 1885 to 1892 and captained the New Zealand side to Australia in 1893. Eyton rated him second to none among the Native team forwards. But it was as an administrator that he made his lasting contribution to the New Zealand game. At various times a selector and member of the management committee of the Wellington Union during the 1890s, Ellison played a major part in the first annual general meeting of the New Zealand Rugby Football Union following its establishment in 1892. It was on his motion that the meeting adopted the now legendary black uniform with silver fern leaf (the uniform of the Native team) as the national playing colours. Appropriately, he captained the first New Zealand representative team to wear it.

The distinctive and controversial 2-3-2 scrum formation with a wing-forward was another of Ellison's innovations.

It was probably at Ellison's instigation that the Native team gained from his Poneke club another equally talented player, David Gage. A Te Aute old boy, Gage played for Wellington, Auckland and Hawke's Bay in a representative career stretching from 1887 until 1901, as well as representing New Zealand in eight matches between 1893 and 1896. A versatile player who mastered all back-line positions, he displayed a remarkable durability for the Native team, appearing in no fewer than sixty-eight of the seventy-four matches in Britain.

Auckland's North Shore club provided the second set of brothers in the touring party, the Wynyards — George (Sherry), Henry (Pie) and William (Tabby). Pie Wynyard was not an original tour selection. Having gone to Britain on his own business early in 1888, he joined the team at Newcastle in November. He had played no provincial rugby prior to the tour, but made four appearances for Wellington in 1891 and 1892. Sherry Wynyard had no representative record either before or after the tour, but Tabby Wynyard was a sportsman of outstanding ability. A fast three-quarter with a penchant for dropping goals, he played for Wellington and Auckland between 1887 and 1896 and was a leading figure on the New Zealand tour to Australia in 1893. For the Native team he distinguished himself as much for determined play in over fifty of the British matches, as for his frequent singing of "On the Ball", which had been written in Palmerston North the year before the tour. A talented golfer, oarsman, cyclist and billiards player, he also represented Wellington and Auckland at cricket and athletics.

Dick Maynard, another member of the North Shore club without a provincial pedigree, may have gained his tour place at the instigation of the Wynyards, although this is not certain. Nevertheless, he became one of the better forwards in the team and later played for Auckland in 1889 and 1892 and Poverty Bay in 1894.

Teo Rene, who represented Nelson against New South Wales in 1886 and against Wellington in 1887, and Harry Lee, who played for Southland in 1887 and Wellington in 1889 and 1892, were the only other Maori members of the Native team with provincial experience prior to the tour. And it was probably this that brought them to Warbrick's attention. Rene, according to Eyton, "was meant for a parson, if not built for one", but spent much of the tour in friendly rivalry with Dick Taiaroa, "always threatening to knock each other out, but without damaging results". Lee, one of a number of players during the early years who made his mark as either a forward or a three-quarter, was to win particular fame in the tour match against Salford by comprehensively outplaying James Anderton, then regarded as one of the best wingers in Britain. As Eyton put it, "Anderton was capsized in a most unmistakable manner".[2]

Rene's selection may be linked to that of another Nelsonian, Wi Karauria.

Tabby Wynyard. He represented Auckland and Wellington at cricket and athletics, as well as being an accomplished cyclist, billiards player, golfer and angler. Off the field he won fame for his singing of "On the Ball". Rugby Museum, Palmerston North

He had shown impressive skills in appearances for Nelson club during 1887, and this was confirmed by his performances as a forward for the Native team. But during the second half of the British tour Karauria fell victim to tuberculosis and died within months of his return to New Zealand.

Of the six remaining Maori members of the team, it is perhaps significant that three — "Smiler" Ihimaira, Charles Goldsmith (Taare Koropiti) and Wiri Nehua — were selected directly from Te Aute College. If they lacked proven experience, they at least came from the leading Maori rugby school. As it happened, none of them achieved anything significant during the tour. Goldsmith subsequently made five appearances for Hawke's Bay in 1889 and 1890. Ihimaira, a bullocking rather than fast half-back or threequarter, who played three times for Hawke's Bay in 1891, made more of a name for himself off the field than on it. Labelled by Eyton as the Don Juan of the team, he was constantly unfit, and when the touring party returned to Australia in May 1889 he was invalided home.

Only three players, W. Anderson and Alexander Webster of Hokianga and Dave Stewart of Thames, cannot be placed in some sort of selection pattern. Warbrick's letters indicate that he visited Thames as early as March in search of players, and it can be assumed that in these as in all selections he relied on his own diverse playing experience. While Anderson and Webster gave reliable service in Britain, neither played any representative rugby outside the tour. By 1893 both were dead. Stewart, possibly the youngest member of the team and certainly one of the most popular, represented Auckland in 1892 and 1893 and went on to establish himself as a successful racehorse owner near Thames.

In all twenty players were selected for what was originally known as the New Zealand Maori team — the title "Native" being adopted only after the addition of Pakeha players. At least five of the team — Ihimaira, Karauria, Nehua, Rene and Taiaroa — were full-blooded Maori. Fourteen, including the late addition Pie Wynyard, were sons of Pakeha fathers and Maori mothers. The parentage of Anderson (sometimes known as Kiri Kiri) and Goldsmith (Taare Koropiti) is unclear, because of the tendency of some Maori to adopt English names during the late nineteenth century.[3]

That at least two-thirds of the Native team, and about half of the players originally approached by Warbrick, were of Pakeha fathers, suggests that a large proportion of the leading Maori players of the period owed something to a Pakeha link. Exclusively Maori clubs did operate, and a number of full-blooded Maori undoubtedly appeared in Pakeha teams, but they did not attract the attention of selectors at the highest level. That Warbrick was eventually forced to compromise his original plans, is more a sign of the absence of Maori from higher playing levels than of a gap in his knowledge of the game. Even with part-Maori players, the pool of talent was not large. Aside from a late attempt to lure Jack Taiaroa, no other effort was made to find Maori players or to change the minds of those in the Wairarapa before Pakeha were added to the team.

It has always been maintained that there were four Pakeha in the Native team, and that Warbrick was prompted to add them after a heavy defeat at Auckland on 7 July. Yet biographical details leave no doubt that there were in fact five Pakeha — George "Bully" Williams of Wellington, Bill "Mother" Elliot, Mac McCausland and Charles "Barlow" Madigan of Auckland, and Pat Keogh of Otago. McCausland's obituary refers to him as one of five Pakeha, and Elliot made the same point when interviewed in 1954.[4]

Obviously these selections were necessary to strengthen the Native team and create a more effective combination. But it is equally clear that they were not forced on Warbrick by defeat at Auckland. Williams was reported as joining the team on 22 June 1888 — one day before the first match of the tour against Hawke's Bay and hence before any weakness in the team could have become evident. The inclusion of Elliot, Madigan and McCausland, the leading Auckland backs, was announced on 8 July, the day after their province's victory over the Native team. Some prior negotiations are likely to have occurred. McCausland, for one, needed time to arrange twelve months' leave from his job with the Bank of New Zealand. The timing of the announcement also allowed Warbrick no opportunity to search beyond Auckland for suitable Maori players, suggesting that he probably saw little reason to do so. The final Pakeha addition to the Native team, Pat Keogh, is more easily explained: he joined just before the team's departure from New Zealand as a welcome replacement for Warbrick who had been badly injured in the match against Auckland.

Apparently the only other player, besides Jack Taiaroa, to be approached by Warbrick was John Webster, a Pakeha who represented Auckland from 1880 to 1883. Having declined a New Zealand tour place in 1884 because he was unable to obtain leave from his job as Town Clerk of Devonport borough, he was still unable to accept when Warbrick extended an invitation four years later.

In the following weeks the addition of Pakeha players caused a good deal of comment and controversy. But for the moment they added much needed strength to the Native team. Williams, a policeman and at thirty-two the oldest member of the team, had appeared seven times for Wellington in 1886 and 1887 and once for Hawke's Bay while stationed at Hastings. Although he did not play rugby until the age of twenty-four, his height, weight and strength were ideally suited to the forward play of the period. He also captained the Native team on several occasions in Britain.

McCausland, a talented three-quarter and the most reliable goal-kicker in the team, played for Auckland in 1886 and 1888 and made five appearances for Hawke's Bay in 1887. Later he was to play twice for New South Wales against Queensland in 1891, and as a first-class referee he achieved distinction by sending off New Zealand's William McKenzie ("Off-side Mac") in the second match against New South Wales on the 1893 tour. Madigan, a brilliant attacking player and the fastest winger in the Native team, was also prone to injury. After breaking an ankle early in the tour, he missed many matches in Britain, although he did return to play. He made nine appearances for Auckland between 1886 and 1890, but his career was cut short by illness and he died at the age of thirty. Elliot, who joined him in the Auckland back-line in 1887, quickly established himself as one of the best half-backs in the colony, maintaining this form throughout Britain. He played twenty times for Auckland between 1887 and 1896, frequently as captain. An original selection for Ellison's 1893 tour to Australia, he was forced to withdraw due to work commitments. At the time of his death in 1958, Elliot was the last surviving member of the Native team, having outlived Dick Taiaroa by four years.

Pat Keogh, another to make his representative debut in the 1887 season, made his mark as one of the most gifted, colourful and ultimately controversial figures of early New Zealand rugby. Unanimously regarded as the best back in the colony, he played a leading role in Otago's one-point loss in their second match against the 1888 British team. Legend has it that Keogh, who missed the

Patrick Keogh, star player, leading try scorer and seldom shy of controversy on and off the field. Keogh was one of two members of the Native team born overseas — in Birmingham.
Irwin Hunter, *Rugby Football: Some Hints and Criticisms*

first match supposedly through illness, was in fact watching it through a hole in the Carisbrook fence and planning his strategies against the visiting back-line. In Britain his fleet-footed play took him to the top of the Native team try-scoring list with thirty-four. But his career ended prematurely in 1891 when the Otago Rugby Union banned him on charges of gambling and professionalism. Although reinstated in 1895, he did not play again.

With the inclusion of Pakeha players, it was decided to change the name of the team from New Zealand Maori to New Zealand Native Football Representatives. Eyton justified this on the grounds that all members of the team had been born in New Zealand. But evidence shows that McCausland was born in Gippsland, Australia, and Keogh in Birmingham, England.[5] It is extremely doubtful that Warbrick, Eyton and Scott remained unaware of these details, especially in the case of McCausland who came to New Zealand at the age of fifteen. The title "New Zealand Native Football Representatives" was therefore more of a promotional device than a genuine reflection of its content.

In its final form the team consisted of twenty-six players. While accurate dates of birth can be determined for only twenty of these, the average age was twenty-two or twenty-three, with Williams the oldest at thirty-two and Webster or

Stewart the youngest at eighteen. Motives for joining the tour seem straightforward. It is commonly held, and there is little reason to doubt it, that virtually all were single and "stony broke" and had little in the way of good jobs or family obligations to keep them in New Zealand. The prospect of adventure on an all-expenses-paid trip to Britain and Australia must have been a great temptation. The possibility also exists that some stood to gain financially from the tour.

When it is remembered that modern All Black teams for long tours number thirty players, and that the 1992 All Blacks in Australia and South Africa called on no fewer than thirty-six, a touring party of twenty-six was not a large one. Moreover, it included the almost permanently injured Joe Warbrick, and Pie Wynyard who did not join the team until its fifteenth match in Britain. Yet the original plan was for an even smaller touring party. In May Warbrick had named twenty players as certain to tour, and said that two more would be added. By July, with the inclusion of four Pakeha players and Maynard, and the withdrawal of Jack Taiaroa, Warbrick had settled on twenty-four. The late addition of Keogh boosted the team to twenty-five when it left New Zealand in early August 1888.

In part, such a small touring party was normal for the time. The New Zealand team to Australia in 1884 numbered only nineteen, and Seddon's British team for a much longer Australasian tour in 1888 contained twenty-one. It is also likely that Warbrick's selection difficulties restricted numbers, and that the promoters sought to reduce costs by taking the smallest possible team. At the end of the tour Scott was very critical of some players and declared that they could easily have managed with an even smaller party. To the contrary, events showed that a larger party would have solved many problems and avoided much hardship.

By the beginning of May 1888 most of the Native team had assembled at Warbrick's home base near Napier. Having rented a house and employed a cook, they spent a good deal of their time training and exercising. Some members also made appearances for the Hawke's Bay County Football Club, causing objections from other Napier clubs but not from the Hawke's Bay Rugby Union which declined jurisdiction on the matter. The itinerary being arranged for the tourists was extensive. They would travel via Melbourne and Suez to Britain, thereafter playing twice a week for six months before returning to Australia for further matches in May 1889. As it transpired, these plans were to grow still further.

In the eyes of Warbrick, Eyton and Scott, the team contained an ideal balance for what lay ahead. It possessed a core of experienced and talented provincial players and a number of others with considerable potential. At the same time the predominantly Maori composition of the team would appeal to public curiosity. The interaction of these two elements played a major role in shaping the tour.

3
The honour of the colony

Although difficulties lay ahead, the relationship between the Native team and the New Zealand provincial rugby unions was at first fairly smooth. The unions were willing to organize matches against the team, and to assist them with fifty to sixty percent of gate takings from these matches. Even if the tour was not under their control, they saw little reason for alarm during its early stages. Consequently Warbrick had no difficulty arranging matches against Hawke's Bay, Auckland, Nelson, Wellington, Canterbury, South Canterbury and Otago.

Writing in early June, the Southland player, Harry Lee, predicted a bright future for the team: "The men appear to be on the whole a quiet sober lot and they all get on well together."[1] When interviewed about the strength of the party, Warbrick was certain that they could hold their own against any

The Native team cap, the first appearance of the silver fern in New Zealand rugby. Ron Palenski

opposition, being good tacklers and possessing what he considered to be the best back-line in the colony. He said that the opinion in some quarters that the forwards were weak was not justified and could be attributed to the fact that good players such as Maynard, Webster and Karauria were not well known outside their own districts.

The Native team approached their first match against Hawke's Bay at Napier on Saturday 23 June 1888 with some confidence. Although the team had not yet been strengthened by the Auckland Pakeha, it included eight players with provincial experience — Ellison, Rene, Taiaroa and Williams in the forwards, with Joe and Billy Warbrick, Gage and Tabby Wynyard contributing to a strong back-line.

In front of 1,000 spectators — a good crowd considering the Napier population of 7,700 — the tourists dominated both halves of a hard, fast match and won 5-0, with tries to Tabby Wynyard and Ellison and a dropped goal to Gage.* While the win was not as large as some had expected, and there was a lack of combination among the forwards, it was enough to impress a local reporter.

> The visitors were much heavier all round than the local players who, with one or two exceptions were all light men though speedy ... The second spell was as hard a bit of football play as the district has seen for a long time, the play being of determined description and all over the ground, the distinguishing feature of both sides being the passing of the team ... Judging by the play in this match, Warbrick's combination will give provincial clubs some work to do.[2]

One week later the team again met Hawke's Bay. With three changes to the forwards, the margin of victory was increased to 11-0. Fred Warbrick scored a try from half-back and Joe Warbrick contributed the remainder of the points. Immediately after the match the team was farewelled from Napier with a well-attended dinner at the Criterion Hotel. One participant described the scene:

> The dining room ... [was] crowded with an enthusiastic gathering of footballers, ex-footballers, would-be footballers and admirers of the game one and all anxious to do homage to those who were so soon to do battle for this colony on English soil.[3]

For the match against Auckland on 7 July the Native team was at nearly full strength, but their opposition was formidable. Along with Elliot, Madigan and McCausland, who were soon to join the touring party, Auckland included T.B. O'Connor and John Lecky, who had toured Australia in 1884, and Rab McKenzie who was to tour with Ellison's team in 1893. Even then, some felt that this was not the strongest team the province could field.

But Auckland had learnt a lot from their matches against the British team

---

* Except in New South Wales and Queensland, tries counted one point, conversions two points, and dropped goals and goals from marks three points.

in May, and they produced a scientific performance against a hapless Native team which scrummaged badly and lacked penetration in the backs. If a loss by five tries to nil was bad enough, it was made worse by a serious injury to Joe Warbrick who suffered several broken bones in his foot during a tackle. He was not to play again until November, and he never regained his best form at any time during the tour.

After the match one local reporter offered a scathing assessment of the touring team.

> Taken collectively the Maoris are a poor team ... They lack combination, are very poor at packing the scrums, and the majority of the backs are indifferent at picking up ... I think that if such a team goes to England a false impression will be conveyed of the rugby game as played in New Zealand. It is pretty certain that as at present constituted, there are several senior clubs in the colony who could beat them.[4]

Earlier doubts about the strength of the forwards were certainly coming true, and it was clear that the team needed much more training together. Yet, reinforced by Auckland players, they were to perform far more convincingly in their remaining New Zealand matches, losing only to a strong Otago side on 28 July.

However, other problems began to appear after what had been a relatively uneventful beginning to the tour. Just before the first Hawke's Bay match there were signs of disharmony between the players, the promoters, the press and the provincial rugby unions. It also became apparent that some observers attached a significance to the tour which lay far beyond the rugby field, a significance which the Native team did not always appreciate.

Some within the rugby fold regarded sport not as a matter of simple pleasure, but an activity capable of shaping politics, opinions and national images. Joe Warbrick himself wanted to lift Maori rugby to the status attained by Australian cricket, and others saw a similar aim for the Native team. From the early 1860s onwards, Australians had made much of the role of sport, and especially cricket, as an indicator of the healthy qualities of people in their new colonies. Cricket victories over England in 1876-77, and even more importantly those on English soil in 1878 and 1882, gave many Australians a feeling of reassurance. Although they were no longer living in Britain the Mother Country, they had proved themselves in ways that were important to their British counterparts. Above all, they had not deteriorated in a distant land renowned for its harsh climate and convict origins.

There is a similar tone to an early assessment of the Native team offered by "Threequarter-Back", the football columnist for *The Press*.

> The visit of the first football team from New Zealand to the Home Country is an event which is certain to be regarded with great interest by every colonist of both races, and the result of their doings in England is certain to be watched with

interest equally as keen as that which attended the matches played by the Australian cricketing team.[5]

Another Christchurch columnist, writing in *The New Zealand Referee,* praised the composition of the team and predicted a promising future for them in Britain.

> It must certainly be admitted that no fault can be found with the representative nature of the team, almost all parts of New Zealand having a representative to do battle for them, and although they may be beaten in their international matches against All England, Scotland and Ireland, still I predict a most prosperous career for the Maori "reps" and feel certain that victory will follow them in the majority of their matches.[6]

On the other side, critics were soon to pursue their case with even greater intensity. Within New Zealand it was easy enough to explain any indiscretion by the Native team, on or off the field. They were after all an unrepresentative team outside the control of rugby officialdom. But a British public who did not know the truth about its origins would regard the team as a product of New Zealand and as indicative of its rugby and its social standards. It was essential, critics argued, that players exhibit the highest standard of behaviour in all places and at all times.

The position of the provincial rugby unions on questions of behaviour was very clear. During the 1870s some critics had regarded rugby as an anarchic and violent pastime. When a player was killed in a club match in 1877, the coroner declared that the game of football was "only worthy of savages". And the following year *The New Zealand Herald* claimed that "bull-baiting and cock-fighting have more to commend them as recreations than the rough and tumble hoodlum element yclept football which our youths seem to take so much delight in".[7]

During the 1880s the unions rapidly moved to organize and control the game. Team sizes and playing times were standardized, referees were given much greater jurisdiction on the field, rules were modified to encourage an open game which relied more on skill than brute force, and disciplinary procedures were set in place which applied equally off the field as well as on it. Indeed, seven of the twenty-six clauses of the first New Zealand Rugby Football Union constitution were devoted to discipline. Severe penalties were introduced designed to discourage gambling, professionalism and any form of lavish expenditure on the entertainment of players. Although the new code was not completely set in place by 1888, it nevertheless made a strong showing as the Native team plunged into controversy on several fronts.

The first dispute struck directly at the heart of rugby officialdom and triggered precisely the reverberations they had been striving to avoid. On 22 June, the day before the first Hawke's Bay match at Napier, *The New Zealand Referee*

The New Zealand Native team. There is no single photo of all members of the team. Pie Wynyard is absent from this group. *Rugby Museum, Palmerston North*

reported a major disagreement between the Native team players and promoters concerning terms of payment during the tour. An unnamed source stated that in addition to first-class hotel accommodation while in Britain, the players were to receive twenty-five percent of all tour profits after expenses. The report stated that some players felt that this left too great a share for the promoters, Scott and Eyton, and that several were threatening to leave the team.[8]

Where this report came from is unknown. If a dispute actually existed, it was soon resolved because there were no subsequent changes to the team aside from the addition of Pakeha players. Yet the implications of such a report were very serious. Although it was acceptable to pay basic travel and living expenses while on tour, any direct payment for playing the game was strictly prohibited. In accordance with the position held by the Rugby Football Union in England, New Zealand officials were equally determined that their game was to be played by amateurs for their own pleasure and not for monetary gain.

But increasingly the views of the gentlemen amateurs who controlled English rugby had come under threat, and the Native team could hardly have picked a worse time to test their resolve. Throughout the 1880s working-class clubs, especially in Yorkshire and Lancashire, had been allowing "professional" elements to enter the game. A pattern developed of clubs enticing good players, mainly Welshmen, with jobs and other incentives. Some also sought to compensate players for earnings lost while playing or while injured as a result of playing. Such payments were called "broken-time" payments, or "boot money". Only seven years after the Native tour these issues contributed to a dramatic split in British rugby which produced the Northern Union game, the forerunner of modern rugby league.

However, in 1886 the Rugby Football Union had shown its determination to stop such practices and to preserve the amateur game. New laws stated that players found to have taken payments for playing were likely to be expelled from the game. Two years later further laws were made to control the transfer of players between clubs, curbing the practice of enticement. At the same meeting in 1888 the Union, which had not sanctioned the visit of Seddon's British team to Australasia, banned one of its players, J.P. Clowes, for allegedly accepting payment of fifteen pounds from one of the tour promoters for clothing and other items. Concern was expressed that other members of the team had also infringed the laws, and all were required to provide an affidavit stating that they were receiving nothing other than necessary expenses for the tour. This document having been provided, the issue was apparently resolved, although not for Clowes who accompanied the team throughout Australia and New Zealand without being allowed to play.

Thus the question of professionalism was very much in the minds of the New Zealand rugby fraternity when the *Referee* published its report on 22 June. Strangely, though, the provincial unions did not react quickly and at least three weeks passed without any public comment or question from them. The sporting press, on the other hand, were in no doubt about the action that ought to be taken against the Native team. "Threequarter-Back", who emerged as a persistent critic of the tour, insisted that measures be taken to avoid embarrassment for the players and, more importantly, to preserve the standing of rugby in the colony. He demanded that Warbrick and the team provide a declaration, similar to that of the British team, stating that they were not professionals. Moreover, "Threequarter-Back" felt, the provincial unions should insist on such a document before giving their support to the team or playing further matches against it.

> Wellington, Otago and Canterbury are affiliated to the Rugby Union and being on the spot the committees of these provincial unions should see to it that the team does not go Home under false colours. If it does, the players will certainly be disqualified by the Rugby Union and the good name of the unions here will suffer. The duty of requiring the declaration may involve unpleasantness, but it is a duty and in honour should be discharged.

The *Referee* columnist was equally certain that action should be taken. He said that his original report had been published only to highlight and clarify the issue of professionalism before the team left New Zealand. In light of the Clowes case it would be unfortunate and embarrassing if the Native team undertook the long and expensive journey to Britain only to be banned when they arrived.[9]

Warbrick's response to these allegations was swift. On 6 July he forwarded a reassuring telegram to the Canterbury Rugby Football Union. "Absolutely no foundation re charges of professionalism against Native team. All travelling on bare expenses. Circulated reports are made through jealousy." When the team arrived in Christchurch two weeks later, Warbrick announced that all of them had signed a deed of arrangements, drawn up by a Hawke's Bay solicitor, stating that they were not professionals. He also explained that the reports of professionalism had been circulated by a Christchurch gentleman who had wanted to take the running of the tour away from Eyton and Scott and join with the promoters of the British team. Without a doubt Warbrick was referring to Mr Brown, whose overtures he had declined in May.[10]

With this explanation, and Warbrick's legal document, the *Referee* declared that the case was now closed. But Brown was not alone in his views, and there is certainly room to pose further questions regarding professionalism.

Arthur Shrewsbury, one of the promoters of the British team, had a definite opinion on the matter. In two letters to his English business partners, in May and June 1888, he expressed considerable surprise that the Rugby Football Union had extended its patronage to the Native tour. "Talk about a speculation," he wrote on 15 May, "there is one with a vengeance and for the Union at home to give their support, after refusing us, is a clincher — but I imagine they will want to know something more about it before the matches are arranged." Three weeks later he was more direct in his accusations. "These men are professionals hundred to one more than Clowes and all of them I believe have arranged as to the terms to be paid them."[11] Shrewsbury was well acquainted with arranging tours and his comments, given in private correspondence, are more credible than if they had been offered directly to the press. But having already expressed regret at not making his own offer to Warbrick, his comments may also have been coloured by the same jealousy as Brown's.

When the Native team reached Britain at the end of September 1888, Eyton sent an emphatic denial to George Rowland Hill, secretary of the Rugby Football Union.

> Dear Sir — In accordance with the wishes of your Union as stated to Mr J.A. Warbrick and myself at a meeting last Friday, I write to say that we are prepared to submit our account for inspection should you desire at any time for the purpose of making it plain that no member of the team with which we are associated has received or will receive any remuneration for his services beyond his bare travelling expenses.[12]

With this and with the "deed of arrangements", it is possible that Warbrick and Eyton were calling the bluff of the Union, trading on the fact that true gentlemen would take them at their word. Then again, there were severe consequences for taking such liberties with a body renowned for its extreme sensitivity on matters of professionalism. In the long run the Union accepted Eyton's assurances quite readily; indeed, it was reported on several occasions after the team arrived in Britain that the Union was entirely happy about its amateur status. Earlier in the year the *Daily News* had described the tour as:

> ... a strictly amateur business, contrasting sharply with the tour that some English players are about to commence in New Zealand and Australia. We hope the New Zealand players will be properly representative of the strength of the colony, if so, the visit is sure to be a great success.[13]

A leading administrator and rugby historian of the period, the Reverend Frank Marshall, described as "an ardent upholder of the amateur ethos and witchfinder-general when it came to rooting out transgressors of the transfer laws", was also quite sure that the Native team were not professionals and cited their offer of accounts to support his case.[14]

Still questions remain. Although an inspection of accounts would confirm whether money was being paid to players during the tour, there was no real safeguard to stop profits being distributed at the end. In fact this was a common form of payment on many cricket tours where it did not became clear how much was available to be divided until all expenses had been settled at the end of the tour. Secondly, with their basic expenses covered none of the players stood to lose from the tour, but one wonders how willingly they would have played simply to line the pockets of Eyton and Scott without receiving anything themselves. Warbrick's position here is also ambiguous. On the one hand he was a player supposedly bound by the amateur code, yet he increasingly became an organizer closely associated with the finances of the tour.

Whatever the truth may be, there was an immediate consequence for the Native team. Although the Rugby Football Union found no problem with their amateur status once they reached Britain, those who witnessed the earlier stages of the tour in New Zealand were still inclined to view it with a good deal of suspicion. Their tolerance was to be tested even further when a second major controversy erupted, this time concerning the addition of Pakeha players to the touring party.

One Pakeha player, George Williams, joined the team the day before the first match at Napier. In view of what followed, this caused no initial reaction other than a rather cynical quip from the *Canterbury Times*: "How he hopes to pass muster we cannot say, unless it is by a liberal application of walnut juice. Perhaps he will remain a pakeha and go to England as a representative of the athletic colonial youth."[15] Ironically Williams, at thirty-two, was the oldest member of the team.

By mid-July critics were less inclined to be flippant. The addition of three further Pakeha — Elliot, Madigan and McCausland — provoked immediate hostility. Having supported the tour, the press now declared that a Native team with Pakeha players was a direct threat to the authority of the provincial rugby unions — a position which equally implies that a team *without* Pakeha players was *not* a threat. On 20 July the *Otago Witness* presented the case in these terms:

> If these men are to be allowed to play, there is nothing to hinder Warbrick from picking up good men from each of the provinces and making the team a New Zealand one. If a New Zealand team is to go home, well and good, but by all means let it be a thoroughly representative one and in that case it should be a team sent home by the New Zealand unions and not a money-making venture promoted by Messrs Warbrick & co.[16]

At the same time the Otago Rugby Football Union announced that it was reluctant to play against a Native team with Pakeha players. Soon after, the Hawke's Bay Union passed a motion condemning the inclusions: "[T]his Union considers the addition of Europeans to Mr Warbrick's Native team injurious and encroaching upon the functions of the various rugby unions in New Zealand." A further motion was foreshadowed: "That in the event of Mr Warbrick taking Europeans to England to play in his Native team, the Union withdraw its patronage." This motion did not proceed, although the Union did send a letter to Warbrick instructing him to tell those in Britain that the team was not generally representative of the colony and that the Pakeha had only been added in an emergency due to a shortage of suitable Maori talent. Otago, after a strong warning to Warbrick that his inclusion of Pakeha was in breach of an earlier agreement, also decided to proceed with arrangements for its matches.[17]

An original agreement that the team would consist only of Maori players, suggests that they were viewed differently from Pakeha. Hawke's Bay certainly implied that a Maori team did not pose any threat to their authority. Why this distinction should be made is not clear from available evidence. The furore over professionalism had shown that the unions were quite willing to exercise control over their players, and it seems only logical that this should have extended to Maori. Indeed, in the nineteenth century the view of Maori as possessing an inferior moral character and standard of behaviour was very widespread. With seven Maori members of the team having played provincial rugby, and all others having appeared for Pakeha clubs, the unions could hardly claim that these players were outside their jurisdiction.

Whether Eyton's desire for a Maori team had anything to do with the ambiguous stance of the unions is unknown. Both he and Scott had wanted a purely Maori team, but had discovered that "with a due regard for the decent dignity of the rugby game", this was impossible.[18] This at least confirms Warbrick's limited selection possibilities and the tenuous grounds for selecting a Maori team in the first place.

Some in the press felt that a team containing Pakeha players would not be an attractive or lucrative spectacle in Britain. As the *Taieri Advocate* put it:

> Lovers of the sport at home will not take nearly the same interest in the doings of the visitors as were the team composed wholly of Maoris or half-castes; consequently the attendances of onlookers will certainly not be so great. The advent of a native team would be sure to draw well in any of the large centres of population — whether able to conquer or obliged to accept the position of the vanquished. But when one knows that the title of the visitors was a misnomer, the reverse would assuredly apply.

In this were echoes of the earlier views of Maori players in the Wairarapa. The *Referee* also suggested that if Warbrick was going to include Pakeha players, he should cooperate with the unions to select a team that would be fully representative of the colony. This would "prove a much greater success ... at home than the present half and half team".[19]

It is doubtful whether the press were really interested in the financial viability of the tour. Rather, they were more concerned with the image the team would leave behind in Britain. While there was no complaint about the composition of a Maori team, the addition of some Pakeha players quickly drew demands for a fully representative team that would do justice to the colony as a whole. A "half-and-half" team, should it not succeed, ran the risk of showing its Pakeha members in a comparatively bad light. A purely Maori team would avoid that risk.

In spite of these controversies, the team began to combine together on the field and achieve consistent results. After leaving Auckland they encountered bad weather and were obliged to spend a rough night on their steamer before being able to land at Nelson on 11 July. Nevertheless, on a very wet and muddy Trafalgar Park, seven tries were scored without response from Nelson. But according to a local correspondent the play was not of the highest standard.

> The match did not offer a good exposition of football, though much amusement was afforded the spectators by the floundering of the footballers ... The chief characteristic of the Native's [sic] play was their passing and combined play.[20]

In this game the Native team set an unfortunate precedent in that only one of the seven tries was converted — by Wiri Nehua who kicked only one more goal on tour. (Of the 337 tries scored by the team, only 122 were converted, a success rate of only thirty-six percent.)

Three days later, on 14 July, with Elliot and Madigan now having joined the tour, Wellington was defeated 3-0 through a dropped goal to Tabby Wynyard. In a further twist to the player controversy, it was reported that Jack Taiaroa had agreed to play against Wellington on condition that the Native team was purely Maori. With Elliot and Madigan in the side, he did not play — which leaves a question as to whether university commitments were his only reason for declining a tour place.

On 21 July, on a hard and dry Lancaster Park, and in front of a large crowd including many Maori from Kaiapoi, Canterbury were defeated 5-4 in a keenly contested match. This was followed by a comprehensive 9-0 victory over South Canterbury on 24 July. By all accounts the match was memorable for brilliant back play from the Native team, although the back-line in question contained Harry Lee and Arthur Warbrick, who usually appeared as forwards, and Smiler Ihimaira who was never renowned for his pace.

Otago, on 28 July, were an altogether more difficult proposition. Aside from Pat Keogh, the home team contained nine players who were to appear for the South Island against the British team in September 1888. Among these were T.W. Lynch, whose son and grandson each represented New Zealand, and Alex Downes who became a noted referee and also represented New Zealand at cricket from 1895 to 1907. Although McCausland made his first appearance for the Native team, the loss of Joe Warbrick had obviously caused disruption, and his brother Arthur again appeared in the backs. Like Auckland, Otago had learnt much from their two matches against the British team and won easily 8-0 in a fast and open game.

For the return match three days later, the Native team adopted a far more conservative wet-weather approach to win by a single try to nil. But their methods did not produce a great deal of admiration.

> The game turned out to be as slow and as uninteresting as Saturday's game was fast and exciting. It consisted of a series of tight scrums, the Natives having learned on Saturday that they were no match for the Otago men in the loose play. They kept the ball continually in between the first and second row of their forwards,

and if by chance the ball did come out of the scrum, the gigantic and genial Smiler was there to fall on it.[21]

A year later Otago supporters would praise the Native team for their fine running game.

Thus at the end of the first leg of the tour, the Native team had recovered from the humiliation against Auckland. They had won seven of the nine matches, and gradually found confidence and combination. But the Canterbury and Otago matches gave rise to a new set of objections to the tourists, this time concerning their sportsmanship and attitude to match officials. In Christchurch, "Threequarter-Back" felt that the Native team needed to "play more according to the rules" and that Fred Warbrick, especially, was guilty of offering unwarranted advice to the referee. Four days after the match against Canterbury, and after further criticism, the football columnist offered an explanation for his views that was to be repeated several times during the tour.

> I dwell at this length on the bad points because the team will to an extent carry the honour of the colony in their hands at home, and even if their play does not improve their spirit must do if they are to avoid rough games with some teams that doubtless they will meet, and do credit to followers of the game here.[22]

During the first match against Otago the team again drew a hostile response for its playing methods. As *The Press* described it, "The game was an exceedingly rough one. The Native team seemed determined to win by fair means or foul. Downes and Croxford were both kicked on the head rather badly, the former having rather a bad cut."[23] When the team reached Britain, similar complaints came close to ending the tour.

Thus, after promising beginnings, the Native team which ended its first New Zealand tour was under some criticism. Motives for the tour were suspect, a taint of professionalism was in the air, and the sporting conduct of the players was far from acceptable. As far as the press was concerned, the team was not ideally suited to convey a healthy picture of New Zealand to British eyes. On the other hand, although the provincial unions threatened to take action, they never withdrew their patronage for the tour. Nor did they approach the Rugby Football Union with any of their concerns. Perhaps some in rugby circles were simply over-sensitive rather than genuinely worried.

In time the Native team would be welcomed by many Britons while greatly antagonizing others. They would walk a fine line between the two bitterly opposing camps of British rugby and, as far as the authorities were concerned, end up in the wrong one. But immediately ahead lay Melbourne, Suez and a British itinerary that would eventually amount to an exhausting seventy-four matches in six months. And when the tour ended in Auckland more than a year after their departure, the team had played over one hundred games.

4
"Maori enough"

As the Native team embarked at Dunedin for Australia on 1 August 1888, they were an unknown quantity venturing into an unknown world. There was no way of knowing how effective their play would be in Britain, or even what teams they would be playing against. From a British point of view the visitors were equally mysterious. New Zealand was at the farthest end of the Empire and reliable information about it was limited. More importantly, few non-white people had been seen in Britain, and only a handful of Maori had visited during the previous eighty years. What would they look like? How would they play rugby? And how civilized would they be?

The first port of call for the Native team was Melbourne, where Eyton, Warbrick and Wiri Nehua had travelled a week earlier. Melbourne was the bastion of Victorian (Australian) Rules football which had been established during the late 1850s. The Victorian Rugby Union was only formed when the Native team returned to Australia in May 1889. But Scott was keen to establish contacts within the Victorian Rules community. If the Native team could be trained in the local code, there was considerable potential for gate money from matches against the leading Melbourne clubs when the team returned to Australia.

With this in mind, Scott engaged a Victorian coach, Jack Lawlor, to assist with his plans. Lawlor was a good player for the Ballarat and Essendon clubs and had been to New Zealand in May 1888 to assist the British team with their own attempts to learn the Victorian game before they returned to Australia. Unfortunately, the crowded itinerary in Britain was to give Lawlor little time for coaching. Eyton, who left for London a week ahead of the team and did not know about Lawlor's addition to the party, regarded him as an expensive liability.

On this first visit to Melbourne the Native team played only two games — both under rugby rules against the Melbourne Rugby Football Club. In the first, in front of more than ten thousand spectators at East Melbourne on 11 August, the visitors won easily with tries to Keogh, Ihimaira and Lee. In the return match, a fourteen-a-side encounter on 15 August, they were surprisingly held to a draw, each side scoring one try. Nevertheless, the team had made themselves known in Australia and Scott had undoubtedly established useful contacts.

Native team "play up" card. These were always popular collectors' items for sporting enthusiasts. Ron Palenski

From Melbourne the touring party embarked on a six-week steamer journey to Britain via Suez. It was planned that they would maintain fitness on board ship by a rigorous training routine and by stoking the coal-fired boilers. However, the disturbance to other passengers and the liberal sprinkling of coal dust in the ship's bathrooms soon produced a ban on these activities, in spite of Scott's protests to the captain. Hence the only available exercise was a scratch game of rugby while the ship was waiting at Suez. As Eyton recalled, "[this] was probably the first time the game was played in Egypt — there being no mention of the game in ancient history".[1] But the stop also produced a casualty when Rene seriously injured his foot while bathing in the canal. Although the nature of the injury is not recorded, he did not play until the twelfth match in Britain.

When the team reached Tilbury Docks, London, on 27 September 1888, they were not in peak physical condition. According to *The Sportsman*, their arrival "caused much curiosity and the natives who carried some relics of their race in the shape of spears & c. were surrounded by crowds of spectators". *The Daily Telegraph* offered a much more colourful welcome.

> We have been invaded, and the Maori is upon us. Full five-and-twenty strong he landed at Plymouth, moved to Fenchurch St and is now encamped at Richmond, busily preparing and practising for the forthcoming fifty or sixty pitched battles to be fought in the course of the coming season. Yet the timid may take heart of grace; this invasion of peaceful and pleasant character threatens no new danger to England ... It is but another of those ever-welcome colonial invasions in which our fellow subjects from across the sea come to wage friendly war with us in some of our national sports and pastimes ... The Maoris have

"Maori enough"

certainly progressed since Captain James Cook ... found the finely painted and neatly tattooed ancestors of our visitors eating each other in the bush.[2]

Such overtones of savagery and references to cannibalism were just the sort of publicity that Eyton and Scott were looking for.

The team were met by Mr F.W. Burnard of the Rugby Football Union and a Mr Olivey of Surrey, and taken to the Greyhound Hotel, Richmond, to prepare for the opening match of the tour against Surrey on 3 October. Coincidentally, this was the same day that the British team played their last match in New Zealand. In all, fifty-two matches were originally arranged in England, Ireland and Wales. Owing to friction between the English and Scottish unions, only one match was arranged in Scotland — at Hawick on 22 November. Subsequent invitations to play Edinburgh University and other Scottish clubs had to be declined due to lack of space in the itinerary.

Although without Tabby Wynyard, and Joe Warbrick, who was still injured, the Native team for the Surrey match was a strong one. On taking the field, they became both the first team from New Zealand to perform a haka and the

"The Surrey team cheering the 'Maories' on their appearance", before the opening match of the British tour. This is from a set of six illustrations relating to the Native team which made up the cover of the *Illustrated London News* on 13 October 1888.

first to play in a black uniform. The *Illustrated London News* described them thus: "They are dressed in black knickerbockers and jerseys, which in the case of the Maoris, with their dusky hue of face and hands, gives them a rather sombre aspect".[3] The jersey bore a badge incorporating goal posts, a ball, a fern-leaf and the motto "Play up New Zealand".

In front of a crowd variously estimated at 5,000 and 50,000 the Native team completed an efficient, if unspectacular, victory. Goldsmith scored the first try in Britain, which proved to be his only one of the tour, Ellison added a second and McCausland kicked a conversion. Throughout the game the team remained on amicable terms with the referee, Mr George Rowland Hill, secretary of the Rugby Football Union.

The Times was quick to remind its readers that Surrey was only a scratch team, and the result did not necessarily mean that the Native team would beat strong clubs or international sides. But it added that they were opponents worthy of respect, and had played well considering they had only been in Britain for a week. Moreover, the London public had quickly warmed to the visitors.

> The first appearance of the New Zealanders created no little excitement in the football world and Richmond was invaded by upwards of 50000 [sic] visitors, all anxious to witness the debut of the antipodeans. The leading lights of the Rugby Union fully atoned for their absence from Fenchurch St to welcome the Maoris on their arrival by attending the first match in large numbers. The enclosure was thronged by eminent footballers, while nearly all of the members of the Australian cricket team put in an appearance.[4]

If victory over Surrey caused a certain amount of surprise, the next two, especially that over Kent, were even more unexpected. Against Northamptonshire the tourists' back-line ran in five of the six tries, including two each to Madigan and Elliot, in an easy 12-0 win. Kent, however, were a much stronger combination. In front of a large, partisan crowd on a cold afternoon at Blackheath, they offered the stiffest resistance of the three teams met so far. Success was eventually achieved through tries to Keogh and Arthur Warbrick, and the local press offered an encouraging assessment of the performance.

> This stamps them as a far stronger team than they were first supposed to be, and when they learn to pass more, they will want a lot of beating. As it is, they seem to rely on their forwards, and from what I have seen I think they are by no means ignorant of the tricks of the game, as some of their friends have told us.[5]

The surprise results now took a twist in the other direction, as the team narrowly lost to both Moseley and Burton-on-Trent. These teams were from an area near Birmingham that was dominated by soccer, and most assumed that the visitors would win with ease. Unfortunately the Moseley match produced a spate of injuries, with Billy Warbrick (broken collar-bone) and Sherry Wynyard (ankle) suffering the most. At one stage the Native team were reduced to only eleven men on the field, there being no provision for replacements. In explanation of the next match, at Burton-on-Trent, Eyton mused that "meeting residents of the famous brewery town, it is not much to be wondered at that we allowed the quality of English ale to excel the colonial and retired with our second defeat".[6] Whether this hinted at things to come is not clear.

Amends for these setbacks came in the form of a solid victory against a weak Midland Counties side at Birmingham on 20 October. Fred Warbrick and Elliot scored tries and Tabby Wynyard and McCausland landed dropped goals. The result did not please some of the local gentry who had been confident enough to offer two to one odds on the Midland side.

So far the team had won three and lost three with the prospect still awaiting them of some very difficult matches in Yorkshire and Lancashire. Yet their performance in the next match, against Middlesex County at Sheffield Park on 22 October, must have caused Eyton and Scott grave concern.

The Earl of Sheffield was a noted sporting enthusiast who had done much for Sussex cricket and had hosted matches against the Australian touring teams of 1884 and 1886. Therefore, although Middlesex was not on the original fixture list, the Native team gladly accepted such a significant invitation. It was originally intended that Rowland Hill would arrange a scratch team for a festival match, and that was the impression held by the Native team when they reached Sheffield Park. However, the organization of the home team quickly passed to the Middlesex Union which raised a county side including several England, Scottish and Welsh internationals. Entrance to the match was by invitation only and the spectators included many notable social and political figures.

The task facing the Native team was now formidable, and it was made even more so by events before the match. Two hours before the start of play both teams were treated to a full luncheon, including wine. The result, for players unaccustomed to such luxury, was fairly predictable. As the correspondent for the *Lyttelton Times* put it:

> English footballers are accustomed to smart lunches on special occasions before the game commences, and take good care to be strictly abstemious. To the Maoris, however, the departure was a new one and it cannot be denied that they innocently made the most of the many good things that Lord Sheffield's genuine hospitality provided.[7]

When both teams were later assembled for a photograph, it was found that two members of the Native team were missing. They were soon located sleeping in a shrubbery.

Once on the field, the play of the touring team was, in Eyton's words, "void of combination, though individuals played well".[8] In spite of a promising start they were quickly on the defensive and conceded three easy tries during the first

The *Illustrated London News* artist's impression of the first goal for the Native team, being scored by Charles Goldsmith. Goldsmith did not score again until the team returned to New Zealand.

half, mainly as a result of poor tackling. The second half was marked by brilliant solo efforts from Madigan and Elliot, but neither scored. Middlesex added a try and a dropped goal to their total, eventually winning 9-0. Against their strongest opposition and the most prominent audience of the tour, the Native team had done nothing to enhance their reputation.

But at least one member of the team felt that there were grounds for complaint.

> If the Moseley match was rough, I should like to know what term to apply to the Englishmen's play at Sheffield Park. We went down there for the lunch and a jaunt. The match was to be a secondary consideration. What we expected was a moderate opposition and a mere exposition of "the noble game of football". I, for one, thought the match would develop into a free fight.[9]

As the Native team left London for Yorkshire, some in the south of England, such as Rowland Hill, may already have been forming the distinctly unfavourable impressions that were to produce a great deal of hostility later in the tour.

Eyton preserved this account of the Middlesex match in *Rugby Football Past and Present*.

NATIVE TEAM V. MIDDLESEX

Maclagan set the game in motion on behalf of Middlesex from the western goal at seven minutes past three. The New Zealanders quickly showed to the fore, and in the course of the first few minutes were very conspicious by several good rushes, in which they used their feet well. Inglis then headed an effort which carried the fight well within the visitors' lines, but the ball was touched down. Roberts put in a rattling run, but made a bad pass, or a try must have resulted. Directly afterwards, however, Lindsay got possession from a line-out, and dribbled the ball over the line, securing the first try for Middlesex about eight or nine minutes after the start. Johnston took the place, but did not improve upon the point. The visitors continued to act chiefly on the defensive, Cousins being conspicuous in a couple of splendid rushes, while Inglis, Hammond and Surtees were always well on the ball. After another seven or eight minutes had elapsed, Roberts received the leather from a smart pass by Gould, and running right through the Maoris' defence, grounded the ball behind the Colonists' goal, Johnston on this occasion having little difficulty placing a goal. Anderson on re-starting put in a fine run, but the Maoris replied with a counter-effort on the part of Gage and Keogh, though they were palpably outplayed in every department of the game. Gould and Lindsay made a pretty combined effort, Inglis from a line-out carrying the ball still nearer the New Zealand goal. A scrummage followed, after which Maclagan made a plucky attempt to drop a goal, but the only result was a minor point. [A minor was a defensive touchdown. Like the modern tight-head count, it was noted, but not part of the official score.] The next noteworthy feature was a good dribble by Hedderwick and Hammond followed by a splendid bit of combined passing in which almost all the Middlesex backs had a hand. Just before half-time Inglis got possession and transferred to Anderson, who made a grand run and wound up with another try, which Johnston failed to convert, and when the whistle sounded the interval the score stood at a goal and two tries to nil in favour of the metropolitans.

Play for the first few minutes in the second half was carried on in the vicinity of the centre line. Lindsay, who had not been shining too brilliantly, made a capital drop, but the only result was another minor. The Englishmen continued to hold the upper hand, and Anderson, after a scrummage, put in a rattling run which ended in a fourth try, Johnston again failing with the shot at goal. On resuming, Keogh made his mark, but at too great a distance to prove dangerous. Gould tried once or twice to get away without success, and then Elliot put in a splendid rush, but was collared, when he looked like getting in, by Surtees. Madigan twice made dashing but fruitless runs, but the county would not be denied, and continuing to press, and Lindsay, from a distance of about thirty yards, dropped a splendid goal. The only other items were a brilliant run by Madigan, who all but scored, and a further minor registered against the New Zealanders, who were defeated in the end by two goals, three tries, and five minors to nil.[10]

Thus the first month of the tour was marked by erratic results on the field. It also produced some interesting reactions off it. Elements of the British press and public, unaccustomed to non-white visitors on their own soil, initially treated the Native team with a good deal of curiosity, commenting on their appearance, language and behaviour. Others, as "Threequarter-Back" had predicted before the team left New Zealand, viewed them as having much more than a sporting purpose.

When international cricket between England and Australia rapidly expanded during the 1870s, some in Britain began to discuss the value of sport for establishing common standards and holding the far-flung British Empire together. Indeed, Lord Harris, the doyen of English cricket administrators, believed that the game of cricket had "done more to draw the Mother Country and the colonies together than years of beneficial legislation could have done".[11] Harris and other old boys of elite British public schools felt that the discipline, cooperation and conformity needed to achieve good results on the field led to similar habits within society as a whole. The common bonds of sport, as well as English language and literature, went a long way to explaining how Britain was able to maintain control over such a large empire with only a small military presence.

It was believed that the process would achieve even more if the indigenous peoples of the Empire — Maori, Aborigine, Indian, African — could be taught British games. This would break down cultural differences and encourage cooperation. In India the princes were encouraged to take an interest in cricket, polo, billiards, hockey and various forms of football. There, and in the West Indies, schools were established along the lines of the British public schools to foster loyalty to Britain through education and games. In Australia, some missionaries encouraged Aboriginal cricket for the same reasons. And in New Zealand, Te Aute College and other schools attended by members of the Native team, had used rugby to establish common ground between their Maori students and Pakeha.

The day after the Native team arrived in London, *The Daily Telegraph* assessed their visit in glowing terms.

> The spectacle of the noble Maori coming from different parts of the earth to play an English game against English players ... is a phenomenon that is of the very essence of peace and bears a message of kindly import and good-will towards men.[12]

The morning after the opening match against Surrey, a leading article in *The Times* offered the best explanation of the importance of the tour.

> From one point of view it is a tribute to our colonising faculty. The colonising race that can imbue the aboriginal inhabitants of the colonised countries with a love for its national games, would seem to have solved the problem of social amalgamation in those countries ... Wherever the Englishman goes he carries the bat and the goal posts ... [T]he first leisure day in an invaded colony is sure to bring forth its cricket match or its athletic sports, in the latter of which, at all events, the natives with that touch of nature which makes the world akin, take a fraternal interest ... The popularity of our English games in the colonies is a striking phenomenon. It forms a bond of sympathy between the various parts of the Empire of which, perhaps, the strength is as yet imperfectly realised.[13]

Lord Harris and "Threequarter-Back" could not have faulted such sentiments, which established a sporting link with New Zealand seventeen years before the 1905 All Blacks.

"Maori enough"

Outside London the press carried nothing to match these views. Newspapers in small towns, such as the mill and mining communities of Yorkshire and Lancashire, were so parochial in their coverage of sporting events that most did not even publish the results of the international against England on 16 February 1889. Their only interest in the Native team was when it arrived in the district for a particular match. Perhaps, then, "Threequarter-Back" and others were exaggerating when they claimed that "those at Home" saw a wider meaning in the Native tour. More likely, the only ones concerned were a select group of public school old boys in London.

Others were preoccupied with the "Maori" aspect of the team. Although there had been some black slaves in London during the eighteenth century, and small communities of foreign seamen, students and traders had appeared by the 1880s, few in Britain had seen non-white people at close quarters or knew anything about the distant lands they came from. Most based their ideas on books which contained inaccurate information and sensational illustrations. Indeed, in 1878 at least one observer was considerably surprised that the touring Australian cricket team were not black like their Aboriginal predecessors of a decade earlier. With this level of knowledge and contact, it was easy for speculators to make money by parading various "natives" before a fascinated public. For, as one writer observed, "falsehood feeds on the credulity of the ignorant".[14]

The few Maori visitors to Britain during the nineteenth century, such as Moehanga of the Ngapuhi in 1807 and Hongi Hika in 1820, all attracted considerable attention. Each was granted a Royal audience, as was Tamihana, a son of the famed Te Rauparaha, in 1852 and the group of "chiefs" toured by William Jenkins in 1863-64. In 1829-30 Whiti and Ariki Toa of Ngati Maru were toured as a commercial venture — with posters claiming that both had partaken of human flesh.

But these visits were hardly regular enough to fill a gap in British knowledge of the Maori. When the Native team arrived in Britain there was much comment about their appearance and behaviour, as if the public were unsure of what to expect. Shortly after the Surrey match *The Field* declared itself impressed with the look of the team. "It was evident to the merest tyro that our visitors lacked nothing in point of physique, their appearance betokening both strength and staying power, two things quite essential to the successful playing of football." The *Illustrated London News* described them as "all men of fine growth, well knit and well proportioned", and the *Daily Telegraph* saw them as "finely built men with characteristic olive complexions, bright brown eyes, singularly white teeth and it may be said that they have agreeable voices and pleasant manners". After the tour, "Bully" Williams recalled similar impressions from the British press. "It was humorously stated in English newspapers that the

Maori players had abnormally well developed legs and especially feet, and therefore the centre of gravity being low down they took a good hold of the ground and were hard to upset."[15]

A writer in *The Times* was disappointed that the team did not live up to a rumour that they would play without boots, and said that they did not look significantly different from an English XV on the field. "But the strain on the whole is Maori enough to have offered a sharp contrast of complexion and build to their opponents yesterday — a contrast which was by no means all in favour of the Englishmen." And when the team went to Hawick for their only Scottish match in late November, the local reporter showed a mixture of surprise and admiration.

> They were as fine a body of stalwart, muscular, athletic men as anyone might wish to meet ... They are not unlike Europeans, that is the resemblance is great when one remembers that they were a savage tribe no further back than a generation, perhaps.[16]

Contrary to expectations, Britain had discovered that the Native team were both civilized and conventional in appearance.

Only one paper, *The Dewsbury Reporter* from Yorkshire, was not impressed. "Taken as a whole their physique is by no means as impressive as one would suppose from the expressions of the press, indeed some of them are absolutely small and by no means superior to the average local player."[17] Perhaps there was a point to this: the "average player" in Yorkshire, as the Native team soon discovered, was in fact bigger and more skilful than in many other parts of Britain.

Another feature which particularly bemused spectators was the performance of the haka. Scott announced before the tour that the team would perform a haka prior to each match and that they were taking elaborate mats and other traditional costume to embellish the performance. However, the response to the first haka before the Surrey match was not encouraging. "The Native team appeared in their mats and gave their war cry — Ake Ake Kia Kaha — which little pantomime was somewhat ridiculed by the English press and the mats were afterwards discarded." The *Sporting Life* described the haka as "a 'whoop' in the vernacular which caused great amusement", and a leading rugby administrator, Frank Marshall, saw it as nothing more than a gimmick which was soon abandoned. "[W]hen the real merit of their play was recognised, they discarded these advertising spectacles and depended upon their genuine exhibition of football to attract spectators."[18]

The Sydney *Bulletin*, in its usual colourful fashion, was also cynical about the haka and other Maori elements of the tour.

> The Maori football team in England appear to combine the best elements of a football team and a circus. When they go on the ground they have their mats and rugs on and they dance a war-dance and sing a war-song before beginning play.

"*Maori enough*"

This intimidates the other side and attracts huge piles of gate money. The Maori umpire, instead of the normal walking stick that umpires use, carries a war club. The British spectators sit by in a flutter of excitement, expecting him to dash out the brains of some of the players on the slightest sign of a dispute. Of course the show draws like a mustard-plaster and the promoters ought to make heaps of money.[19]

If it did not appreciate the cultural significance of a haka, the *Bulletin* understood the objectives of Scott and Eyton better than most.

Some observers were also amused by the use of Maori language on the field, while the team gained their own pleasure from listening to personal remarks about themselves made by people who presumed that they could not speak any English. But all of these responses to the team were more a matter of ignorance and misunderstanding than any kind of deliberate racism. As with the Aboriginal cricket team who had toured Britain twenty years earlier, the press reported only one racial slur during the whole tour. Following the match against Rochdale on 18 March 1889, the local players "all most positively asserted that they would not play against the 'darkies' for no one, for they say they are only half

Unaccustomed to Maori visitors, the press had ample opportunity to play on British imagination.
Illustrated London News

"Their war cry before starting play". The first haka performed by a New Zealand rugby team in Britain, during the match against Surrey, 3 October 1888. *Illustrated London News*

civilized".[20] Even then, part of this might have been a reference to rough play. Those who criticized the haka had nothing but praise for the manners and playing skill of the visitors, and although they were to run into many controversies during the tour, the players themselves retained only fond memories of the way they were treated by ordinary people off the field.

For all of this comment, it seems that many observers found that the Native team was not as "Maori" as they had expected. *The Times* remarked on the European presence in the team, but concluded that they were "Maori enough". *The Field* noted the Maori and European parentage of most of the team and informed its readers that only two "natives", Wi Karauria and Dick Taiaroa, had appeared in the opening match against Surrey. And *The Sportsman* was in no doubt about the nature of the team. "The term 'Maori' as applied to this troupe of rugby union players is something of a misnomer seeing that the combination consists of but six pure Maori, fifteen half-caste and four [sic] New Zealanders."[21]

Eyton recalled the situation quite clearly.

> The British public no doubt expected to find the Maori football team (as it was so often called) to be composed of black fellows, and as we could not show anyone darker than Smiler, Karauria, Nehua, Taiaroa and Rene, who can only be said to be badly sunburned, it looked almost like a fraud to expect the British public

"Maori enough"

to believe such as the Warbricks and the Wynyards & co. to be typical of the Maori race. We had not even a tattoo mark among the team, and in their walks abroad they attracted little or no attention from the casual passer-by.

On one occasion in early November, to keep faith with the expectations of the public, members of the team purchased black masks and wore these as they arrived at a railway station in northern England. The reaction is not recorded.[22]

After only a month in Britain the Native team had come to be noticed far more for their football and far less as a Maori curiosity. There was a wide gap between British expectations of "black fellows" and a team of whom less than a quarter were full-blooded Maori. Perhaps their being a rugby team also helped to alter public perceptions. Instead of being seen as savage and cannibalistic, they were regarded as a group of Maori who played a very British game in an entirely orthodox fashion.

"Punch" welcome to the Native team

You've come then, brother Maoris,
at us to have a shy
And if we'd guard our glories
we'll have to mind our eye.
Our camp you seem to flurry,
and stir its calm content
You've flabbergasted Surrey,
and scrumpulated Kent.
Your kicking, brother Maoris,
has given us the kick,
You're well matched all, well "on the
 ball"
And strong and straight and quick.
By jove this is a rum age,
when a New Zealand team
Licks Bull at goal and scrummage;
it beats McCauley's [sic] dream.
You're welcome, brother Maoris,
Here's wishing you good luck.
With you there pace and power is
and skill and lots of pluck
A trifle "rough"? Why, just so?
but that you'll mend no doubt
And win, all sportsmen trust so,
in many a friendly bout.

Quoted by *The Press,* 9 January 1889, p.5.

5
Players, profits and promoters

The easy acceptance of the Native team mainly as rugby players posed a problem for Scott and Eyton. The team were now left to draw crowds largely on the basis of their playing merit, and attempts to exploit their cultural attraction were unlikely to succeed. As attendances and gate receipts fluctuated the tour was extended and the promoters demanded more games against better teams. By early November tensions were developing and the tour was becoming something less than a happy adventure.

With their move north from London in late October, the Native team encountered the toughest opposition of the tour. For although English rugby was controlled by public school and university men in London, its playing strength during the 1880s lay in the northern working-class areas of Yorkshire and Lancashire. After the establishment of the county championship in 1888-89, Yorkshire won seven of the first eight and Lancashire won the other. The pattern was broken only when the north broke away from the Rugby Football Union in 1895. Before the split Yorkshire alone contained more than 150 clubs, almost a third of the number affiliated to the Union. Indeed, rugby was so popular and important to northern communities that in Yorkshire local derbies attracted 6,000 spectators at a time when international matches in London were drawing only 4,000. As a rugby league historian explained the appeal, "The populace, released briefly of a Saturday afternoon from the mind-numbing drudgery of mill and mine, derived pride, pleasure or pain from the exploits of their local team".[1] Not surprisingly, Scott quickly recognised the financial potential of the north for the Native team and did all in his power to concentrate their matches in that area.

The first five matches in the north produced mixed results — two wins, two losses and a draw. But it could not be said that the Native team were playing badly. The narrow losses to Hull and Wakefield, each by a try to nil, were against strong sides from famous clubs which to this day continue to exert a powerful influence in the rival code in the north of England. The victory over Dewsbury on 27 October was especially meritorious, because the local side contained a number of internationals, including R. E. Lockwood, one of the best three-quarters in Britain. Against this opposition, injuries to Ellison, McCausland and

Tabby Wynyard restricted their participation for large parts of the match. Nevertheless, resolute defence by the Native team held their opponents scoreless. With the wind in their favour late in the game, McCausland and Wynyard ensured a win with long-range dropped goals.

Moving further north at the beginning of November, the team gained the first draw of the tour in a game against Northumberland County at Newcastle. In this match Billy Warbrick made a welcome reappearance in the back-line only three weeks after breaking his collar-bone against Moseley. Two days later, on 5 November, a second-string combination, including Goldsmith making a rare appearance at half-back, easily accounted for Stockton-on-Tees with converted tries to Elliot and Lee. Next came Tynemouth, and although the victory was easy enough, the match was more important for the first appearance on tour of Joe Warbrick. Playing at full-back to test his foot injury, he succeeded only in aggravating it and did not take the field again for two weeks.

The team was about to embark on a streak of seven successive wins, but first they suffered their heaviest defeat thus far, losing 4-13 to Halifax Free Wanderers on 10 November. While conceding only two tries to one, the visitors were undone by three dropped goals to the Halifax backs. Eyton noted that the injury toll was rising, and several key forwards missed this match.

The immediate response of the tourists was to achieve their biggest winning margin in Britain, scoring five tries to trounce Newcastle and District 14-0 on 12 November. As Eyton remarked, "Smarting under the last defeat, our boys fairly romped home winners."[2] And this remained the pattern for the next fortnight as twenty-two tries were scored in six matches and only four were conceded. Cumberland County gave away six, Carlisle R.F.C nine (but only two were converted), and East Cumberland five.

These matches also contained plenty of incident in other respects. The weather at Carlisle on 20 November was so bad, with wind, snow and lightning, that the team tried to persuade Scott to postpone the match. In the end it became a farce as three of the Carlisle team and Keogh were too cold to take the field during the second half. With the wind behind them and overcoats draped around their shoulders, the Native team had little difficulty scoring tries.

An unknown member of the team provided this account of the match for Eyton.

NATIVE TEAM V. CARLISLE

From a correspondent within the Native team.

Yesterday was an awful day. During the forenoon the wind blew bitterly hard and cold, and in the afternoon it grew even worse. At 2 o'clock lightning lit up the gloomy sky, and thunder mingled with the howling wind. Presently, too, sleet began to fall and pile up in gutters and corners. Those of us elected to play were quite dismayed by this weather and begged Scott to postpone the game for another day; but he was inexorable and declined to hear of any delay. So, our boys feeling utterly miserable and out of spirits, were driven to the ground in a storm of sleet. No time was lost in getting ready for the toss, and our opponents elected to play with the wind at their backs. The snow had stopped for a few minutes when we entered the field, but no sooner did we kick off than a great mass of clouds discharged their hail-like contents slap in our faces. It was cold. We tried to smile at one another, but could only manage to horribly contort our faces.

Our opponents, with the storm in their favour, pressed us at first, but we gradually drove them back. From midfield Ellison carried the ball into their 25, but was collared, and by some accident had one of his teeth broken off near the gum. Shortly afterwards, Williams, Ellison and another dribbled the ball over the goal line and, Williams falling on it, scored a try. McCausland took the kick at goal, and managed to pilot the sphere over the bar. A little later Ellison again put in a good dodgy run, and got in again behind the posts. Mac, however, failed to convert. We continued to have all the best of the play, but no further score was added up to half-time.

When the second half commenced, three of the Carlisle team were too stiff with cold to resume. This rather surprised us, as they were playing in what we supposed to be their usual wintry weather; and further, that they had their backs to the wind, whilst we, from a warmer country, and totally unused to such weather, had been playing with the wind and sleet driving bang in our faces. One of our fellows (Keogh) also had to remain under shelter. The game now degenerated into a mere farce. We stood whenever we liked, and our backs stood on the field with their overcoats thrown over their shoulders. When play ceased we had scored a very easy victory by 2 goals, 7 tries and 9 minors to 2 minors. The scorers on our side were Williams, 3 tries; Ellison, 2 tries; Karauria, 2; Wynyard, 1; and Webster, 1. From all these only 2 goals were obtained, as the great hail-fall and fearful wind rendered place-kicking extremely difficult. The opposing team scored two minors in the first half, but hadn't a show subsequently.[3]

Two days later, in weather that had hardly improved, the team played at Hawick, their only match in Scotland. Here they were greeted by a very large crowd.

> Football enthusiasts were down in great numbers, and it seemed as if the entire juvenile population of Hawick were playing truant, for the swarm of youthful football players that crowded round the entrance to the station was enormous.[4]

The match itself was relatively uneventful in spite of the weather. Hawick, including Laing and Burnett who had been with the British team in New Zealand, dominated most of the match and led by a try to nil at the interval. Only exceptional full-back play from Billy Warbrick saved the Native team before McCausland secured a lucky break and provided a try for Keogh. McCausland's conversion sealed the game 3-1, but not before Dick Taiaroa

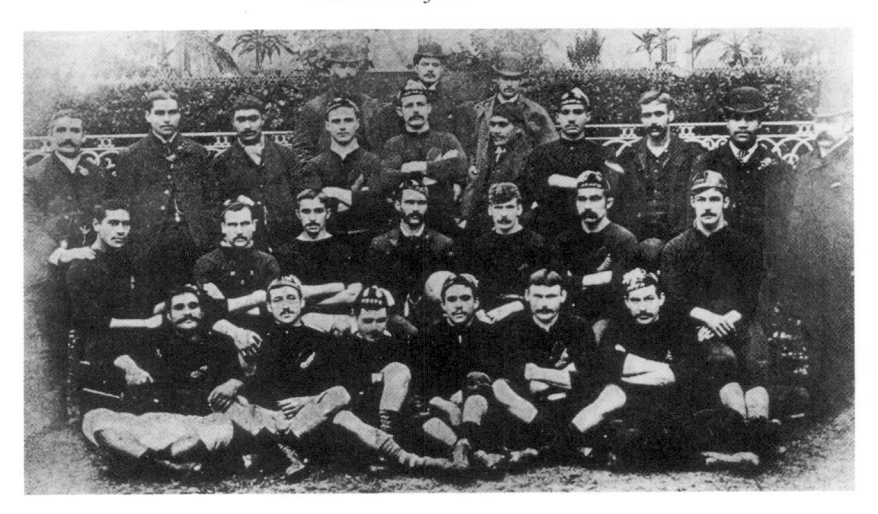

The New Zealand Native team. It is likely that this photo was taken before the Middlesex match on 20 October. Whether it was before or after the team's encounter with champagne is not known.
Rugby Museum, Palmerston North

created a legend for himself in attempting to evade the Hawick full-back. "[H]e threw a kiss to the Hawick back — suggestive of self-confidence in his ability to outpace him — but Riddell responded gaily, and 'grassed' the New Zealander amid tremendous rounds of applause."[5] Proceedings ended with a large and amicable dinner.

Such were the demands of the itinerary being arranged by Scott that the team returned to England on the night of the Hawick match and played games on the next two days, against East Cumberland and against Westmorland County. In the first of these Madigan suffered a broken ankle and did not play again until 12 January. The winning sequence was finally broken on 26 November by a strong Swinton team which triumphed 2-0, mainly due to Valentine their England player. However, seven tries (but only one conversion) produced an emphatic 9-0 victory against Liverpool and District to complete a hectic November. In that month thirteen matches had been played for ten wins, two losses and a draw. December would see another thirteen matches, including two internationals.

Already the tour was making heavy demands on the players. Eyton and Scott were still far from happy with the finances, and this caused tensions with both the Rugby Football Union and elements of the British press.

Large profits from sport were often made during the late nineteenth century. There had always been good money in boxing and horse racing, but it was cricket which really took advantage of major changes in British society. Shorter working hours, higher incomes, a Saturday half-holiday and improved transport and communications all enabled workers to become spectators and their interest in games increased. From 1846 William Clark and his professional All-England XI toured throughout Britain promoting cricket and making their own personal fortunes. Numerous imitators during the 1850s and 1860s did just as well, as did various international touring teams. The first overseas cricket tour, to North America in 1859, yielded £90 for each of its players. On the first tours to Australia in 1861-62 and 1863-64 players received £250 and £475 respectively, although the money-grubbing exploits of the second tour discouraged Australian backing for another venture until 1873.

When tours resumed, Australian crowds flocked to see the new tactics and techniques of players such as W.G. Grace and Alfred Shaw. In 1876-77 James Lillywhite paid his players double their original guarantee, and two years later Lord Harris's team pocketed £500 each. Shaw, Shrewsbury and Lillywhite recouped £750 each as promoters in 1881-82, and a much reduced, but still healthy, £150 each in 1883-84. Australian teams in England fared equally well. Indeed the 1878 team profited to such an extent from their gate money that some English professionals, Shrewsbury included, demanded improvements in their own conditions of employment.

After 1886 there were more failures than successes because of complicated business rivalries and declining public interest. Shrewsbury lost £1200 on a tour in 1887-88, prompting his partner Alfred Shaw to observe that "it was such stupendous folly a similar mistake is never likely to occur again".[6] Shaw still felt that private tours could be profitable; it was merely a matter of appropriate circumstances and careful management. Shrewsbury must have had the same unshakeable faith, because after his big loss in Australia, he stayed there to organize the tour of the British football team, intending to capitalize on the untapped winter market. But this venture also ended in failure, this time costing him £900.

Eyton, Scott and Warbrick were well informed about the possibilities of touring teams, although perhaps more about the profits than the losses. Their London agent, S. E. Sleigh, had managed a private New Zealand team to Australia in 1884, and he undoubtedly provided much useful information about costs and potential gate receipts in Britain. Warbrick had also talked to Shrewsbury at some length when the British team were in Wellington. In common with earlier visitors to Britain, the Native team offered the attraction of being competitive colonials playing British games. Moreover, after a surfeit of Australian cricket teams, they were both the first sports team from New Zealand and the first international rugby team to tour Britain. And at the start of the tour, they had been able to play on the mystique of being Maori.

But very quickly Eyton and Scott discovered the risks of their venture and came to realize that arrangements for rugby tours were far more demanding than those for cricket tours. For one thing, the number of players involved was much greater — twenty-six for the Native team as against fourteen or fifteen for most cricket tours, and only twelve in the case of Shaw and Shrewsbury's first visit to Australia. Besides, the cost of travel was much greater. While the Native team moved their larger party between sixty-one different venues, the 1868 Aboriginal cricket team appeared at only forty-one, and the first six white Australian cricket teams no more than thirty-seven each.

Perhaps the greatest obstacle facing the Native team promoters was that rugby did not dominate the winter to anything like the extent that cricket dominated the summer. Throughout Britain, even in the north, rugby was much less popular than soccer. The administration of Rugby was strongest in the south, but in the north there were no strong public school traditions to promote it. Many working people chose soccer as a more open and less complex game to play. The Football Association was formed eight years before the Rugby Football Union and had established cup competitions long before rugby was properly organized. While rugby internationals in London were drawing only 4,000 spectators, 12,500 saw the first all-northern FA Cup Final in 1884. Interest in soccer was growing at an amazing rate: 27,000 saw a cup tie in 1888, and 45,000 saw the final in 1893. During the next ten years the average attendance at a final was 80,000. It soon became clear that Scott and Eyton did not appreciate that by comparison public interest in rugby was limited.

By Scott's reckoning, the Native team would need to take £100 from each British match to cover costs. The journey to Britain had cost £1550, on top of the cost of assembling the team in New Zealand and securing travel insurance. In Britain there were immediate accommodation, transport and living costs to be met before any return came from the matches.

Eyton and Scott both complained that the hotel bill was double that for similar accommodation in New Zealand. Extras, such as baths, tips and washing, also added up, as did extensive rail travel. Jack Lawlor, the redundant Victorian Rules coach, also cost more than £200.

Against these expenses, returns to the promoters were variable. Arrangements over gate takings were entirely a matter between Scott and the individual host clubs, rather than the Rugby Football Union. Some offered a percentage of gross takings, others a percentage of net, the latter an arrangement which one correspondent saw leading to sharp practice, as there was no common understanding about which expenses were to be deducted first.

The viability of the tour depended almost completely on the number of spectators — and attendances certainly did not meet expectations. In early November Scott said the tour was not reaching projections: it had paid its way and no more. The requirement of £100 a match was not being maintained, and receipts fluctuated greatly. Just before the England international in February, Scott declared that he still needed to recover £1000 before leaving Britain. In a letter to New Zealand the Southland player Harry Lee also expressed disappointment with the gates, saying that the largest attendance was about 8,000.

But the London correspondent for the *Lyttelton Times* felt that the position was not especially bad.

> Mr Scott is not communicative about the financial results of the tour, in fact looks rather gloomy if one mentions the subject. My own impression is that when the accounts are made up at the end of the English tour, there will prove to have been not much in it either way. The promoters may divide £100 or £200 but that's all. I fancy, however, that Mr Scott looks to reap a rich harvest from the Australian matches on the team's return.[7]

Whatever the exact figures were, it is surprising that such a potentially attractive venture did not return a handsome profit. Both the over-optimism of the promoters and a clash of priorities with local administrators had a part to play. Even if rugby was not the main game in Britain, reports of the matches frequently describe attendances as "good" or "large" — 5,000 for Moseley, 10,000 for Lancashire, 8,000 at Wigan, 6,000 at Warrington, 6,000 for the second match against Yorkshire, and numerous others over 5,000. Indeed, the Warrington gate of £148 9s 11d was the second largest ever recorded for that club. Even if these figures are only estimates that may not always be reliable, they at least show that the Native team was attracting crowds that were considered "good" and "large" by local standards. Given the limited popularity of rugby in Britain, the tour seems to have been well supported. Crowds of over 5,000 compared more than favourably with those of 4,000 for internationals during the 1870s and 6,000 for local Yorkshire derbies during the same period.

There is also ample evidence that clubs did everything they could to promote their match with the Native team. The *Warrington Examiner* described the local match on 17 January as the most important in the annals of the club, and Runcorn took a similar view. "It is questionable whether at any time in the history of Runcorn there has been so much excitement as was caused by 'the greatest match of the season'." The match against Barrow-and-District on 17 March was played at 5.15 pm to enable a large number of workers to see it, and on many occasions special trains were arranged to take spectators to matches. The team also attracted considerable support from expatriate New Zealanders and Australians in Britain, one travelling more than one hundred miles to see a match. Such reactions contrast with Scott's gloomy view of gate takings.

At the same time, it must be admitted that the clubs had their own priorities. Most ran a "free list" whereby club members, and in many cases a friend, were admitted to matches without charge. According to Scott, as many as 2,000 were on the list for one northern match, and on many other occasions they turned up in large numbers. In a letter to Yorkshire clubs in late November, he suggested that all members should pay and that usual prices should be doubled for tour matches. But this raised another issue when a reporter at the Huddersfield match said that the attendance had been lower than usual because of the high gate charge. Generally, Scott's request was ignored, and as late as August 1889 the *Otago Witness* noted the effect of the free list in reducing tour profits.

British clubs were more concerned about their members and supporters than about the objectives of tour promoters. Yet when the British team was in New Zealand, clubs' lists were frequently suspended, and even some committee members were obliged to pay. Perhaps colonial administrators were more willing to make concessions to what they regarded as superior opposition from the home of rugby.

The Rugby Football Union were also far from accommodating. Before the England match Scott approached the controllers of the Oval cricket ground and was readily given permission for its use. It was closer to London and better for spectators than the usual international venue at Blackheath. Scott felt that the attendance would be five times as great. The Union bluntly responded that Blackheath was a better playing surface and that they had no intention of sacrificing the match to the gate. Consequently the match was played at Blackheath before a relatively small crowd, although this was partly due to wet weather. Scott mused that if ever he brought another team to Britain, he would organise his own itinerary without relying on the Union who were inclined not to take account of potential gates and such things as travel expenses. For their part, the purists of the Rugby Football Union always insisted that the game of rugby should be played for its own value and not for the interests of spectators or speculators.

Yet the outcome for Scott and Eyton could have been much worse. By fitting in such a vast itinerary, and by attempting to field the strongest and most attractive team at all times, they were at least able to break even. Almost all of the twenty-two matches added to the original fifty-two in the British itinerary, such as those against Newcastle and District, Halifax and Stockton-on-Tees, were in the more lucrative north. In January 1889 Scott tried unsuccessfully to gain release from matches in Somerset and Devon so that the team could find more in Lancashire. His failure was probably due to the intervention of the Rugby Football Union. At the end of the tour he again attempted to profit from the north by arranging another fortnight of matches in Lancashire. This time his obstacle was the Orient Shipping Company, which demanded £100 to change existing travel arrangements to Australia. And it was that company also which curtailed an offer for the team to play matches in South Africa on their return trip from Britain.

Before the team left New Zealand, Scott had raised the possibility of taking a Native team and a British team to Paris to play an exhibition match, and perhaps another in Brussels. But in Britain he had soon discovered that for rugby to be as lucrative as cricket, at a time when the summer game drew huge crowds, he needed a similar number of gate opportunities. Seventy-four tour matches equalled to seventy-four revenue-producing days of cricket. Yet this was still well short of the ninety-nine days of cricket played by the 1868 Aboriginal team, or the 111 of the 1878 white Australian team.

Expanding the tour was all very well, but to draw crowds the team still had to play entertaining and winning rugby. And awareness of the need for gate takings is clearly shown in team selections. In spite of a playing strength of twenty-six, appearances were far from evenly spread. David Gage played in all but six of the 74 matches in Britain, Elliot and McCausland in at least 63, Keogh in 60, Taiaroa in 59, Ellison in 58, Williams in 53, Tabby Wynyard in 52 and Harry Lee in 50. Anderson, Karauria, Stewart, Arthur and Fred Warbrick and Sherry Wynyard also appeared in more than 40 matches. Sandy Webster played in 35 of the first 37 matches before being seriously injured.

David Gage. While all around him were suffering from illness and injury, Gage played in 68 of the 74 matches in Britain. Rugby Museum, Palmerston North

Not surprisingly, thirteen of these sixteen players appear in either Eyton or Joe Warbrick's selection of the best Native XV. Only Karauria and Stewart are not in either selection. William Warbrick and Charles Madigan who appear in both teams, played 36 and 32 matches respectively in spite of severe injuries. Maynard, in Eyton's team, appeared in 38 matches although he too was restricted by injury.

At the other extreme, Alf Warbrick appeared in only four matches, Nehua in eight, Joe Warbrick and Ihimaira in fourteen, and Goldsmith in twenty. Indeed, in a letter to "Threequarter-Back" at the end of the tour, Scott offered a scathing verdict on some of the players. "Mr Scott says that too many men were taken who were not of any use to the team except as ornaments and that they could easily do with fewer men." To the *Lyttelton Times* he described them as "regular dead-heads, their play being of such poor quality that they were only played in the direst extremity".[8] Nevertheless Scott's experience had not dimmed his enthusiasm, and he talked of bringing another team to Britain within two years.

6
Exploits and exploitation

At best Scott and Eyton's attitude to the well-being of the team was uncompromising. At worst it was exploitative. As long as they continued to expand the itinerary and use a lopsided selection policy, injuries were sure to mount and discontent was bound to grow among the players.

During the first three months in Britain thirty-six matches were played in only eighty-seven days, an average of nearly three games a week. In the thirteen days from 22 November to 5 December, eight matches were played, including the Irish international and three matches on successive days. For November and December, the longest break between matches was three days. In addition there were long, uncomfortable rail journeys throughout Britain, a sea crossing to Ireland and the general misery of a British winter, although it was milder than usual in 1888.

Constant playing was common for cricket teams. The Aborigines were engaged for ninety-nine of a possible 126 playing days, and other tourists fared little better. But nineteenth-century rugby was physically very demanding, if not extremely dangerous. The emphasis of the game was still on hard forward play: long and intensive scrummaging and rucking with nine or ten forwards. Much use was made of the "dribbling rush" where the ball was carried down-

Native team season ticket. Ron Palenski

field under the feet of a tight forward pack. Open back play and controlled passing were relatively new and only starting to be refined. Indeed, one observer during the 1880s described backs as "those players who stand at the back of the real action — very handy at times in their own manner, but not really of the essence of the game".[1] The consequences of such an emphasis on hard forward play were reflected in a *Wakefield Express* survey of Yorkshire rugby for the seasons 1890-91 to 1892-93. It reported no fewer than seventy-one deaths, besides 208 broken bones and 158 other serious injuries. There seems little reason to expect different figures for the late 1880s. Not surprisingly, the injury toll of the Native team mounted quickly.

After only three weeks of the tour, Billy Warbrick had broken his collar-bone and the team was hampered by injuries to six leading players. After only fourteen matches, Eyton noted that "our boys were getting shin-sore, stiff and stale".[2], For the match against Westmorland on 24 November, the situation was particularly serious: twelve players were carrying injuries, and Scott was having great difficulty assembling a team. The fifteen that eventually took the field included at least five injured players, and for the game against Liverpool and District four days later the players were described as "a miserable team of cripples". As Joe Warbrick recalled, "Accidents multiplied rapidly, and although we had 26 men in many cases we could not put more than 10 or 12 fairly sound men in the field."[3] More players joined the injury list during December.

A correspondent for the *Lyttelton Times*, who kept in touch with the team throughout the tour, had no doubts about the cause of these problems.

> Five matches in eight days is out of all reason when combined with long railway journeys and the worst possible weather. The Maoris are showing themselves better able to face the conditions of our awful climate than might have been imagined, but they are, after all, only mortal and I am scarcely surprised to learn that on Saturday last the majority of them were in a state of complete physical demoralisation for the time being.[4]

Eyton soon found that his original medical insurance arrangements were inadequate. The company exercised an escape clause after paying out more than £25. The forwards, especially, suffered from bad ear inflammation due to constant scrummaging, and the demand for bandages, plasters and liniment was always high.

> St Jacobs Oil, at first bought by the bottle, was afterwards purchased by the case, and the pungent smell of the embrocation used to pervade our quarters; the spectacle afforded visitors of half-a-dozen men vigorously rubbing each others legs & c. in the sitting room in our hotel must have been rather startling.[5]

There was, of course, no such luxury as a team doctor or physiotherapist.

Inevitably, personal relations suffered under this strain. By December there were reports that several leading players would refuse to complete the Australian section of the tour, and others vowed never to kick a football again once they returned to New Zealand. Much criticism was also directed at Joe Warbrick whose foot injury allowed him to play only fourteen times in Britain. While still team captain, and the logical centre of media attention, some felt that Warbrick took much of the credit for the success of the tour, talked at great length about himself and his brothers, and did not acknowledge those such as Ellison, Gage, McCausland, Keogh and Elliot who played more often. As the *Lyttelton Times* correspondent observed, some players were "a little sore at the constant puffs awarded by ignorant local reporters to Joe Warbrick who had only played twice since the tour began". Furthermore, although Billy, Fred and Arthur Warbrick were very talented players, "it was ... coming it rather strong when the *Star* described Alfred Warbrick as 'the champion New Zealand forward'".[6] He played only four times in Britain.

There was little chance for any of these problems to be resolved. The itinerary for the second half of the tour was marginally more strenuous than that for the first: 38 matches in 86 days, against 36 in 87. When the team was badly beaten in its return match against Yorkshire on 19 January, Eyton had a simple explanation. "The Native team at this time — as at others — was terribly knocked about; and it was scarcely possible to find 15 sound men out of the 26; and such a handicap was too much against such a powerful combination as Yorkshire."[7] A month later, after a week of rest, the team was still described as stale for the England international. Of the consistent performers during the early matches, Karauria, Madigan, Arthur and Fred Warbrick and Webster were now almost permanently on the injury list.

Off the field, matters were no better. Scott declared himself "tired of these football dinners and the subsequent speechifying",[8] and he also became involved in a dispute with Madigan and Keogh who wished to borrow money from him. At the last minute, these two star backs withdrew from the match against Manchester on 11 March and spent most of the afternoon telling spectators that the Native team could not win without them.

Eyton summed up the situation with a warning to future tour organizers which was clearly based on personal experience. "[T]here is the risk of mutinous behaviour on the part of one or more members of the team when fairly started. Sending them back to New Zealand might or might not be a punishment to them, but it would have a disastrous effect on the success of the tour."[9]

Yet most of these details come from the first third of the tour. After November, nine months and more than eighty matches remained before the team finally disbanded, and the pace certainly showed no sign of slowing. But somehow the touring party held together, and the press mysteriously stopped drawing attention to their predicament. There is good reason to suspect that the promoters moved to curb intrusions by the press, especially the *Lyttelton Times* correspondent. Scott and Eyton learnt, as many later rugby tourists did, to keep the media at a safe distance and to conceal controversies within the team. As Eyton knew, sending players home would bring disastrous publicity to a tour, as would letting them talk freely about their problems. This was especially true of a tour which was already viewed with suspicion by many people. Without access to the sympathetic ear of the *Lyttelton Times* correspondent, the players had few alternative responses to the pressures exerted by Scott and Eyton.

A refusal to play was one possibility. If it was not known in rugby, strike action was certainly a part of cricket during the nineteenth century. In 1878 nine professionals from Nottinghamshire and Surrey refused to play against the Australians unless their pay was substantially increased. In 1881 seven Nottinghamshire professionals took the same action against their county committee. More dramatically, in 1896 five members of the England test team struck in protest at their low pay in comparison to the Australian team and the excessive "expenses" being given to amateur players. While pay was not really an issue for the Native team, conditions obviously were.

But any action by the team to cause the collapse of the tour would have left them isolated in Britain. Perhaps only Pie Wynyard, who had gone overseas on his own business, could have covered expenses and secured a return passage to New Zealand without money from Scott and Eyton. The rest, as they had said at the start of the tour, were "stony-broke". Thus the promoters remained firmly in control.

To keep expanding the itinerary when injuries were so numerous, does not reflect well on Scott and Eyton. Were they mainly interested in money? Again, the strongest word on the matter came from the *Lyttelton Times* correspondent.

> The list of fixtures was far too long, which was due solely to the desire of the promoters to make money over the trip without due regard to the wishes of the team. When next a band of footballers leave these shores to do battle on English soil, it should be seen that the engagements are of good number and quality. There should be no risk of having men disabled in small matches which are no credit to win and are only played with the expectation of putting a few pound in the pocket of the promoter.[10]

Even Eyton had changed his mind when he wrote after the tour: "My own opinion is that *to do justice to the team* and the cause of rugby in New Zealand, the next team should not aim at more than 40 or 50 matches in say four or five months."[11] (Emphasis added)

Neither Eyton or Warbrick showed any regret at their lopsided selection policy which created its own share of problems. They proudly boasted that no outsiders were ever drafted into the team, although the offer was made and was sometimes very tempting when the injury list was long. As Warbrick recalled, "I remember at Liverpool we discussed the necessity of picking some outsiders to play for us, but rather than do so Maynard, who was ill in bed, offered to play, also Madigan, McCausland and G. Wynyard who were far from fully recovered from injuries."[12] Even the most obvious replacement, Lawlor the Victorian Rules coach who played some games in Australia, was never used. And ironically he also joined the injury list by falling off a railway platform at Kirkstall after boarding the wrong train.

In the end it appears that the Native team were seen as sportsmen who were quite capable of footing it on equal terms with anyone and looking after themselves. Offers of assistance indicate concern for the players among British rugby followers. But the promoters were determined to maintain the "Native" billing — regardless of the cost, and regardless too of the fact that after the first weeks of the tour the team ceased to be a Maori curiosity. If the team had been more obviously Maori they might have fared better. Previous Maori visitors to Britain, and the Aboriginal cricket team, had attracted much interest from humanitarians anxious that they were not mistreated or abandoned by their promoters. But the reports of the *Lyttelton Times* correspondent produced no outcry in Britain or New Zealand. Perceptions of the team as more Pakeha than Maori set them apart from vulnerable "natives" who could be easily manipulated and exploited.

This, then, was the environment which formed around the Native team by late November, and which continued until their departure from Britain on 29 March. It was not ideal under any circumstances, let alone as preparation for international matches. But that was the lot of the Native team, because in December there were internationals against Ireland and Wales and encounters with two of the strongest county sides in England, Lancashire and Yorkshire.

When they crossed to Dublin on 30 November the team had played thirteen matches in four weeks, and several leading players were carrying serious injuries. Nor were Ireland any better off. Their original selection was beset by injuries, and four more changes were required in the selected XV before it took the field. In spite of these weaknesses, and although the game did not attract the same attention as an England or Scotland international, a good crowd was drawn to Landsdowne Road for the occasion.

Initially the game belonged to Ireland. Early pressure resulted in numerous scoring opportunities and another injury to Billy Warbrick, who suffered constantly as the last line of defence. Finally, late in the half, astute tactical kicking by Walpole gave Waites an easily converted try. Although both Fred Warbrick and Anderson nearly scored for the Native team, the half ended with Ireland leading 3-0.

The second spell began in similar fashion. Constant Irish attacks were met by spirited tackling, but Woods broke through to score another Irish try. At this

The 1889 Ireland team which defeated Wales. Some members of this team took part in the heavy loss to the Native team. Timothy Auty

point Irish supporters were convinced that the match would end in a victory to the home side. But their convictions proved sadly mistaken as the Native team suddenly found form. Firstly Keogh, who constantly amazed spectators with his incisive running, scored two tries, including one from deep inside his own half. Soon after, Williams and Ellison combined in another movement which swept the length of the field and ended with another try. Elliot posted a fourth only a few minutes later. Finally, Maynard broke away to complete another long-range try and McCausland slotted his fourth conversion in a remarkable 13-4 victory.

Naturally Eyton preserved several press cuttings of the dramatic turn-around in Dublin.

NATIVE TEAM V. IRELAND

Considering the recent heavy rains, the sod was in pretty good order, and about ten minutes after the appointed time the Maoris came onto the field dressed in black jerseys and knicks. A very stalwart, formidable-looking lot, too, they were and every man of them seemed as fit as the proverbial fiddle. Scarcely had the cheers which greeted the appearance of the visitors subsided, than the Irishmen entered the arena, and they also received a warm ovation. No time was cut to waste in arranging preliminaries, and, Warren having won the toss, Ellison started the leather at 2.45 against the fairly stiff breeze blowing from the railway end. F. Warbrick immediately led a rush up to the Irish 25, but the Irish team quickly getting together forced their opponents back to neutral territory, where McCausland made his mark, and punted into touch at the home 25. However, a big kick by Edwards completely cleared the Irish lines, and W. Warbrick being tackled before he could respond, the play was at the Maori 25. A clever punt by Walpole was the signal for fierce siege being laid to the goal line, but just as a score seemed imminent, the visitors' forwards rushed the ball away up to Edwards, who checked the stampede in artistic fashion. Scrummaging followed, in which neither side could take the advantage, and then Warren showed up with a useful dribble. Bulger and Stoker were instrumental in placing the Maori goal once more in jeopardy; the last-named following up hard on a loose kick and tackling W. Warbrick close to the line. The full-back got hurt in the encounter, but after the game had been stopped a few minutes he pluckily resumed. Ireland now pressed their opponents very hard and the ball being worked over the line, the visitors barely managed to touch in defence. McCausland dropped out to Walpole, who wound up a dandy run by chucking to Warren, and the later got to the New Zealand 25 before being brought down. Then Jameson might have got in, but preferring to pass, F. Warbrick got hold, and aided by Elliot and Keogh, carried the leather back to the centre. A moment later Warren headed a smart rush to the visitors 25, whence Walpole took a shot at goal and W. Warbrick, in endeavouring to run the ball out, was tackled close to the line. Fierce scrummaging followed from which the oval was shot down into McCausland's hands, and the later promptly making his mark, kicked to Waites, who also in turn claimed a free, which was placed for Walpole. The ball fell short beside the goal post to W. Warbrick, who punted into touch at the 25. After the throw in Warren and Forrest were conspicuous, and a capital punt by Bulger sent the leather into touch close to the visitors' goal line. The scrummage which followed here was of short duration, and after Woods had had a dash at the line, the home forwards were twice in as many minutes nearly rushing the leather over. However, Walpole being charged down in attempting to drop a goal, W. Warbrick brought momentary relief with a strong dash to the centre, and Taiaroa initiated a loose rush, which was neatly stopped by Woods. Then J. Stephenson passed to Walpole, who put in a fine dodgy run to the visitors' 25, and and running and passing between Bulger, Warren and Woods was all but instrumental in lowering the Maoris' stronghold. Woods, indeed, was only pulled down on the line, and soon a shot at goal by Walpole necessitated another touch in defence. Still the score was not long deferred, as Waites, after failing to take a pass from Walpole, quickly got the ball between his feet, and dribbling in fine style, headed a rush on the Maoris' line, outside which he picked up, and grounding the oval behind, gained a try, amidst much cheering. J. Stevenson had no trouble in converting the try into a goal. For a few minutes after the kick off by Ellison the home side continued to have all the best of the game. Lyttle, Forrest and R. Stevenson worked the ball up to the line, and the colonists were glad enough to touch in defence for the third time, but after the drop-out matters underwent a change, and the Maoris showing considerable improvement, began to look really dangerous for the first time during the match. Elliot made a fine run, only being grassed by Bulger close to the goal line, and then a certain score was lost through F. Warbrick failing to negotiate a long pass from Keogh. Bulger at last brought relief with a serviceable punt, and after a determined rush by the Maori forwards had been more than muffled by a grand dribble by Moffat, Anderson, following up on a kick by Gage, got possession and grounded the leather beside the line. This point on appeal was disallowed and half-time was announced; the play being inside the home 25 when the whistle sounded. The second forty was initiated by Warren kicking off to Keogh, whose response was followed by fierce scrummaging outside the Maoris' 25. Jameson coming through had a short dribble which was muffled by a useful run from Goldsmith, but then R. Stevenson dribbled to the verge of the goal, and for some minutes backs had their hands full in the tackling department. First Bulger and then Woods was nearly over, and though Keogh, who was playing a fine game at quarter, gained ground with a punt, a loose rush led by Waites once more caused the Maoris to be hard pressed. Elliot made a plucky attempt to raise the siege, but a fine piece of stopping by Edwards — which he supplemented by a useful kick — once more threw them back on the defensive; and then a beautiful piece of combined chucking and running in which Warren and Woods passed and re-passed to each other a couple of times, resulted in the northern half-back obtaining a try, upon which J. Stevenson failed to improve. The partisans of the home team now considered the match as good as won, but a bitter awakening was in store for them, and between this and the finish disaster followed disaster with most bewildering regularity. The turning of the tide was initiated a few minutes after the recommencement, when Keogh, getting hold near his own 25, had an almost unopposed run in. With the exception of Edwards, who only went for him at the last minute in a half-hearted sort of a way, the entire Irish team — and for that matter most of the Maoris — did not play-on after the appeal for a knock-on, but the try was ruled all right, and our team had only themselves to blame in the matter. It should be a lesson to them in the future not to stop till they hear the whistle; and on the present occasion, as things turned out, it was a very dear lesson. McCausland converted the try into a goal, and the spectators greeted the Maori success with little less warmth than they evinced when the home side scored. From this on, reverse followed reverse with extraordinary rapidity. Elliot and Keogh put in some grand work for the visitors, and the last-named of these, whose dodges seemed inexhaustible, getting possession from a scrummage inside the Irish 25, completely bamboozled Warren by pretending to pass to the half-back, and waltzed over the goal line, McCausland again succeeding to the place. After the kick-off Forrest made a fine dribble, which was only stopped by Warbrick near the Colonists' line; but the ball did not remain here long; for Williams rushing it away up the ground, Ellison picked up and gained the third try, which McCausland missed. The play now became very fast, the home team working very hard to redeem the laurels. The ball was up and down the ground by turns, but the home team returned again and again to the attack. Woods, Walpole, J. Stephenson and Warren were all conspicuous, and eventually W. Warbrick only *managed to avert a score by kicking the ball dead behind. After the drop-out Elliot made a capital run, and a minute later the same player — charging down Edwards close to the goal line — picked up smartly and gained a try, from which McCausland placed an unmistakable goal. Subsequent to the kick-off, Ireland again pressed their opponents hard, and carrying all before them over the line, the leather went into touch in goal. For some minutes subsequent to the drop-out, the Maoris citadel was in constant jeopardy, but the fine tackling of their backs prevented a score more than once when it seemed imminent, and Wynyard at last coming to the relief with a near punt, the visitors had yet another of their tearaway rushes up the field which finished up by Maynard obtaining another soft try. McCausland safely glided the ball over the cross-bar, and a few minutes later "No-side" was called, leaving the Maoris victorious by four goals and a try to a goal and a try.*[13]

Local observers were understandably stunned by the result, but seemed more content to criticize Ireland than to praise the Native team; for example: "That the result shows the home team anything but brilliant scorers goes without saying, and seldom has an Irish international combination shown to less advantage." Another saw the match as "a very poor and easygoing exposition of football throughout, any respectable play being shown by the visitors".[14] But Ireland were good enough to defeat Wales during the same season, and the victory of the Native team should not have been underestimated as it was.

Only two days after this match, with McCausland among others playing in spite of an injury, the team drew with Trinity College. On 5 December they defeated North of Ireland 2-0 at Belfast, and then the party returned to England to face three difficult matches in four days, including both Lancashire and Yorkshire. The most outstanding player in Ireland, Billy Warbrick, had so badly aggravated existing leg injuries that he did not take the field again until 1 January.

Against a strong Lancashire side the tourists were defeated 1-0, although the match was not without controversy. Tabby Wynyard claimed a mark in an ideal position to kick a match-winning goal, but the referee ignored his call and Lancashire were able to scramble out of danger. In this match Pie Wynyard made his first appearance on tour, having joined the team some time before they departed for Ireland.

In some quarters the Lancashire result was seen as justice for what happened in the next match at Batley. Here a weak Native team conceded five tries. Arthur Warbrick, a forward, played in the unusual position of half-back and his brother Alf made one of only four appearances on tour. Thanks to a late conversion by McCausland, the team was able to snatch a draw with only three tries.

Perhaps justifiably, the Yorkshire County committee did not regard the erratic Native team as a major threat to their supremacy: they went on to win

Mobbed. 3 Cheers for the visitors. Hip Hip etc etc.

"3 cheers for the visitors, hip, hip etc etc", at the conclusion of the Surrey match. *Illustrated London News*

the inaugural county championship in the same season. But the county paid a high price for being so confident as to field what was effectively a second fifteen. With Arthur Warbrick again playing at half-back, the visitors scored six tries, and although they yielded four to Yorkshire the 10-6 victory was emphatic. There was severe local criticism of the Yorkshire committee, and they did not make the same mistake for the return match on 19 January.

Comfortable wins over Broughton and Wigan on 15 and 17 December completed a relatively successful fortnight. Finally, Joe Warbrick resumed his place in the side and played in six of the next seven matches before again being sidelined for most of January.

Moving to Wales in mid-December, the Native team set a familiar pattern for later New Zealand rugby visitors by losing to the Welsh. The first victors were Llanelli who won by a single dropped goal to nil on 19 December. Eyton remarked that "Llanelli were jubilant, and treated us with the utmost hospitality, hoping to see us again, which we usually found was the expression when victory rested with our opponents".[15]

Next was the Welsh international at Swansea on 22 December. In a hard-fought match simply described by the local press as "a grand display of football",[16] the Native team succumbed to both superior Welsh play and miserably wet Swansea weather. While they dominated much of the game, and Williams and Tabby Wynyard, especially, impressed with some strong running, the Welsh defence held firm and the few breaks they made resulted in tries — two in the first half and one in the second — for an eventual 5-0 victory. At least the visitors could claim support from many in the 7,000 strong crowd who took exception to there being only one Llanelli player and two Swansea players in the Welsh team.

The press report of the match is characteristically detailed and lively.

NATIVE TEAM V. WALES

The contest between the Maoris and the Welsh internationals came off on the Swansea Football Ground on Saturday afternoon. The match was announced to commence at 2.45, but at three o'clock neither team had appeared on the field and the "gate" was by no means as large as might have been expected considering the interest taken around the event. The places sacred to the sixpenny patrons of football were very much better attended than the south bank, which was reserved for those prepared to pay 1s. About a minute after three o'clock the Welsh team entered the field, looking as fresh as paint in their white pants and scarlet jerseys, and a few minutes afterwards the New Zealanders appeared, and were accorded a very hearty reception. The Maoris were altogether heavier than their opponents, though their black uniform did not show up so well against the green sward as the attractive dress of the Welshmen. As the game proceeded, crowds came trooping in, until the whole area around the field became black with spectators. It was estimated that not less than 7,000 people were present. The kick-off by the Maoris, and the return ... were both fine kicks, and the play for the first minute or so was exciting — the ball travelling pretty well all over the ground. Wales soon extracted a minor from a long kick, and shortly afterwards a loud cheer announced that a try had been scored, and by Towers, who it is said only got into the team by the skin of his teeth. First blood was therefore drawn by a Swansea man. The point was improved upon, Webb kicking a goal from just in front of the posts. The Maoris showed splendid exhibitions of passing, but this did not pay — ground being lost. Soon George Thomas was sent sprinting along, and another try was recorded in favour of the Welshmen. The place kick failed. The Welshmen now showed some splendid dribbling, but this was met by some clever work by one of the Maoris, who played the ball with his knees right across the ground. Play for some time ensued near the half-way flag, but the Maoris by pressure carried the play into the Welsh 25. From a scramble a Maori got across the line, but was carried quite ten yards back into half-way. The advantage, however, was but momentary; the Maoris again pressed, but Stadden relieved, and at half time the ball was in neutral territory. For the last ten minutes the Antipodeans had clearly the best of the game, but the defence of the Welsh was too good to allow scoring.

The second half commenced in a shower of rain, which, with the high wind, rendered the play unpleasant. The proceedings for the first few minutes were uninteresting, the Maoris having slightly the best of the game. The Welsh forwards, however, by a combined dribble, carried the ball into the visitors' 25, but only to have it returned to half way. Shortly afterwards a most exciting piece of play was witnessed. Williams, the mammoth Maori, began a dribble, which was carried over the Welsh line; a try seemed imminent, but George Thomas gaining possession of the leather, by a grand strong run, carried the ball back to neutral territory, where he kicked. The Welsh forwards followed up well, and a try seemed inevitable, but the New Zealanders saved well. Shortly afterwards Nicholls, by a grand dribble, carried the ball across the line. Warbrick tried to touch down, but losing it, Nicholls fell on it and secured a try, which was not converted. The Maoris then made a determined effort to score, forcing the play into the Home 25, but relief soon came. The scarlet and white boys now began to press and Stadden by a grand run, nearly got in. A minute or two later Wales got a free kick, but this was charged down, and the Maoris worked up towards the Welsh goal line, but a Welshman kicked into touch, and time was called, Wales proving victorious by 1 goal, 2 tries, 3 minors, to nil. The cheering which greeted the result was hearty, and the players were escorted from the field by an admiring crowd. Towards the end of the play the light got bad, and it became difficult to distinguish individual players.[17]

On Christmas Eve the team gained their first Welsh win with a convincing performance against Swansea in which McCausland, Elliot and Keogh scored tries. On Boxing Day the powerful Newport side were also defeated in a match which produced one of the largest gates of the tour, more than 8,000 attending. The last match in Wales, and the last of the year, resulted in a 4-1 loss to Cardiff in front of a partisan crowd who gave the Native team "rough" treatment. Immediately afterwards the team left Wales to renew acquaintances with Yorkshiremen.

At the mid-point of the tour thirty-six matches had been played for twenty-two wins, three draws and eleven losses. Among their victories the team could claim such important scalps as Surrey, Kent, Ireland and Yorkshire. Only the losses to Moseley and Burton-on-Trent were against unheralded opposition, and both were at the start of the tour. After a shaky start in October the team had achieved much greater success in November and December and press assessments certainly reflected this change. After the match against Surrey *The Field* had declared that "it may with truth be said that unless they show vast improvement they will find our best clubs too much for them". Similarly, *The Illustrated Sporting and Dramatic News* thought "our visitors, though good, sound players, are by no means phenomenal. A crack team like Blackheath would in all probability prove too much for them". Yet by the end of the year the same

Exploits and exploitation

George Williams. Although he did not play any rugby until the age of 24, Williams emerged as a stalwart of both Wellington and the Native team. Thomas Eyton, *Rugby Football Past and Present*

source announced that having proved themselves in the north the team would be a great attraction when they returned to London, and *The Field* joined the chorus of criticism against Yorkshire for playing a second-string team against such strong opposition.[18]

Contrary to many expectations, there was nothing unusual in the style of play of the team. As *The Daily Telegraph* told its readers:

> The curious ones in the crowd ... who expected some form of unconventional "new departure" were disappointed. They play a fair orthodox rugby game, but nothing out of the common ... Suffice it to record that the New Zealanders have learnt and preserved every rule and tradition of the game.[19]

Most regarded their strength as being in the forwards where they used only eight players instead of the conventional nine. Moreover, they had adopted specialist positions rather than the usual practice of scrums being formed on the basis of first arrival at the spot. The backs, although talented, had a tendency to pass recklessly. In general, though, the team was settling into a sound combination.

7

Gentlemen and competitors

The Native team would have been well advised to savour any praise of their play in the British press. For increasingly the tourists were running into deep conflict with the Rugby Football Union over their vigorous playing methods and forthright approach to referees. They soon discovered that although they played the game in much the same way as many teams in the north of England, their behaviour was not acceptable to the establishment. Accusations of rough play and unsporting conduct, which had simmered since the second match of the tour against Kent, finally turned to dramatic controversy in mid-February.

As in the matches preceding the fixtures against Ireland and Wales, the path to the England international was difficult, especially for a team which was being consistently battered and bruised and becoming demoralised. Nevertheless, of the seventeen matches played before the England game, they won thirteen and drew one. Three of their biggest victories in this period were in the west of England where the opposition tended to be weaker than elsewhere. At the same time, powerful teams such as Huddersfield, Blackheath Rovers, and United Services fell to the Natives who were showing the combination and understanding gained from constantly playing together.

The year did not begin on a positive or friendly note. The attendance for the match at Bradford on New Year's Day 1889 was one of the largest of the tour — perhaps 12,000 — but the lengthy free list greatly restricted the profit for Eyton and Scott. The behaviour of many spectators also concerned them. Twenty-five police were present to keep order, and Eyton feared the worst if the Native team had won the match. As it was, they lost 4-1, and met a now familiar reaction. "The match being over, and Bradford the victors, nothing could exceed their kindness and hospitality. The speeches at dinner proclaimed us all good fellows. &c, &c, ad *nauseam*."[1]

Two days later, against Leeds Parish Church at Leeds, the team escaped with a lucky 6-3 win. While the home side scored three tries, this could not match a converted try and penalty goal by McCausland. On 5 January a rather makeshift Native team, which included rare appearances from Ihimaira, Nehua and Pie Wynyard, managed a convincing 7-3 defeat of Kirkstall. Then followed two relatively uneventful successes against Brighouse Rangers and Huddersfield, and a 3-all draw against Stockport on 12 January. Joe Warbrick made one of his few appearances in this match, but he was described as being very out of form and played only twice during the next month. On the other hand, spirits were lifted by the return of Madigan — against medical advice — after breaking his ankle in November.

Approaching the return match against Yorkshire on 19 January, the tourists had a loss and a win. At Castleford each side scored three tries, but the home team achieved a flattering 9-3 result with superior goal-kicking. At Warrington, where the team met one of their friendliest receptions in Britain, Tabby Wynyard scored a hat-trick of tries in an encouraging 7-1 win.

Now the Native team faced a Yorkshire side determined to set the record straight after its previous debacle. Against a back-line which included such notables as R.E. Lockwood, J.W. Sutcliffe and F. Bonsor, who were soon to play for England at Blackheath, a "terribly knocked about" Native team stood little chance. They conceded three converted tries and a 9-0 lead before Ellison scored in the corner just on half-time. Immediately after the resumption Bradley landed a long dropped goal for Yorkshire and Stadden soon followed with a try. Next, Lockwood evaded Gage, Madigan and Billy Warbrick to run in a sensational try from deep inside his own half, making the score 16-1. But in the final moments Ellison scored his second try and McCausland's sideline conversion made the score a marginally more respectable 16-4. This was by far the heaviest defeat of the tour.

Against Spen Valley four days later, the Native team scored four tries to two, but scraped home by only one point. Sutcliffe, who had kicked four conversions for Yorkshire, was again on target with a conversion and a long dropped goal. Eyton complained that in both Yorkshire and Lancashire, "the clubs ... were remarkably good at ringing the changes upon us by playing the best county men in club matches where we least expected to meet them".[2]

From the north of England the touring party headed to the west country for four matches. For some reason, Eyton described Somerset as second only to Yorkshire in rugby prowess and predicted little success for the Native team. But the complete opposite proved to be the case: on 26 January the team defeated Somerset with their biggest and most stylish victory of the tour, scoring nine tries and winning 17-4. Somerset actually scored first and led 4-0 after exposing Madigan's weakness as an unaccustomed full-back. But Keogh then gave an outstanding display of running, and Gage, Williams and Elliot each scored twice. As the local press enthused, "the passing of the visitors was a treat, while the way in which the whole team played was a noteworthy feature". Eyton felt that moving from the gloom of Manchester had also helped. "The change of climate and quarters had no doubt much to do with their improved form."[3]

Against Devon on 30 January the pattern continued, with another seven tries and Joe Warbrick's only points of the British tour, a conversion. Eyton recalled that "The county of cream, cider and lots of other good things was not very clever at Rugby Football, and the result was an easy victory."[4] Nor were Taunton any better; they succumbed 8-0 on 31 January.

In all the Native team won eight matches in succession between 23 January and 9 February. They overcame a strong Gloucestershire side and a determined Midland Counties team before arriving back in London during the first week of a typically cold and boisterous British February. Their first opponents in the capital, Blackheath Rovers, were despatched with surprising ease. Even without some of their leading forwards, Blackheath had one of the strongest club teams in England. Yet on this occasion their only points came from a converted try to Andrew Stoddart who had recently returned from the tour of Australasia. The Native team won 9-3: Keogh scored twice and Lee and Stewart also scored tries. This game saw the three Wynyard brothers playing together for the only time on tour.

The final match before the England international produced four tries and a 10-0 defeat of United Services (mostly Navy players) at Portsmouth on 9 February. The next fixture was supposed to be against Oxford University three days later, but severe frost and snow caused the match to be postponed for eight days. Thus from 9-16 February the Native team had their longest non-playing period of the tour, the previous longest break being five days between the fourth and fifth matches in mid-October. In scoring terms their preparation for the crucial match was also encouraging — seventy-four points to sixteen in eight matches, and undefeated since Yorkshire.

But there were still problems. For the players, a week was hardly long enough to heal so many injuries. For Scott, there was friction with the Rugby Football Union over the venue for the international match — Blackheath or The Oval — as well as his need to recover costs. For the Union, there was doubt that the match should even proceed, but in the end it did, and at Blackheath, the ground they preferred.

Because of continuing disagreements with the other three home unions — Ireland, Scotland and Wales — this was to be the only international match played by England in 1888 and 1889. Indeed, some felt that the loss of their traditional opponents was the only reason England agreed to play against the Native team. A hotly disputed England try against Scotland in 1884 had prompted the Scots to call for the establishment of an international board to arbitrate and clarify the developing laws of the game. England were adamant that they would join such a body only if they held the majority of votes, a position based on the fact that they had more affiliated clubs than any other union. It was also clear enough that they did not welcome any Gaelic or Celtic threat to their traditional control of rugby. As a result of England's continuing stubbornness, Scotland refused to play them in 1885.

When England refused to attend meetings of the new International Board in 1886 and 1887, the other unions refused to play against them. Not until 1890, after independent arbitration by the president of the Football Association, Major Marinden, did England finally agree to join. The Rugby Football Union held half of the seats on the Board in a system which required a three-quarter majority to pass decisions. But at the beginning of 1889 the Union still held firmly to its notions of supremacy, as the Native team were soon to discover.

Although England named no fewer than twelve new caps for the match, including an entirely untried forward pack, ten were northerners and all were experienced club and county players. Opposing them was a Native team very close to full strength; perhaps only Fred and Arthur Warbrick would have bolstered it. Moreover, in the bitterly cold conditions and on the very heavy ground it was felt that Native team forward power would have a great advantage over fleet-footed English backs who preferred hard, dry surfaces.

The game began, and as expected, for much of the first half strong tackling and scrummaging by the Native team kept England scoreless. What happened next is a matter for much debate. British press reports mentioned disputes between the Native team and the referee, Rowland Hill, but gave no precise details. Only Eyton in his tour book, and Tom Ellison in his *The Art of Rugby Football*, gave full accounts, but their versions are hardly likely to be unbiased. Ellison referred to "distinctly erroneous and depressing decisions of the referee". Late in the first half, Hill awarded two tries to Bedford when first Billy Warbrick and later Harry Lee claimed to have touched the ball dead in goal.

The third decision, shortly after the start of the second half, was altogether more unusual. It began with Ellison attempting to tackle Andrew Stoddart as he ran for the line. Ellison later explained:

> I lured him into my arms by applying the feign dodge. By a quick wriggle, however, he escaped but left a portion of his knickers in my possession. He dashed along and the crowd roared; then suddenly discovering what was the matter he stopped, threw down the ball, and in an instant we had the vulgar gaze shut off by forming a ring around him.[5]

With most of the Native team encircling Stoddart, and believing that he had called "dead ball", they were in no position to stop Frank Evershed who picked up the ball and appeared to score in the corner in spite of a desperate tackle from Madigan. Nor was this the end of the matter. As the Native team vigorously disputed the try with Hill, Evershed took the opportunity to gather the ball and place it under the posts in a better position for Sutcliffe to convert. As Hill awarded this try, Williams, Taiaroa and Sherry Wynyard walked from the field in disgust. Several minutes elapsed before Scott persuaded them to return and finish the match, which Hill had restarted without them. Although the Native

Andrew Stoddart. Captain of the British team for much of its Australasian tour in 1888, and captain of official England cricket and rugby teams during the 1890s, he took his own life in 1915. Rod Chester

team rallied to place England under a great deal of pressure in the final stages, Sutcliffe broke away for another try and eventually a 7-0 win to England.

Assessed more than a hundred years later, events do not become any clearer, although the contrast between Ellison's detailed account and the vagueness of the English press reports may offer some indication. Ellison's view was given some support by at least one prominent member of the Rugby Football Union who was reported as saying that England might have "given way" over Evershed's try.

Ellison was particularly scathing about Rowland Hill, maintaining that his real mistake was more serious than anything he did on the field.

> I may add that gross as these errors were, they were insignificant when compared with another that Mr Hill committed at the outset of the game, viz, refereeing at all in that game; he being the most important official of the English Rugby Union [sic] and the father of the team pitted against us.[6]

This was not to be Ellison's last word on the matter, even allowing that his book was primarily a coaching manual designed to teach the skills and etiquette of rugby.

The Rugby Football Union immediately demanded an apology from the Native team for their behaviour. Accordingly, Mac McCausland, captain in place of the injured Joe Warbrick, forwarded the following telegram from Cambridge on 20 February.

> To Rowland Hill,
> As captain of the New Zealand team I beg to apologise to the Rugby Union committee for the insults offered by my team to their officials on the field of play on Saturday last, and beg on behalf of my team to express their regret for their behaviour on that occasion.[7]

Apparently this was McCausland's second apology. His first had been rejected by the Union who insisted that unless he provided another, at Hill's dictation, the tour would effectively be ended, because players affiliated to the Rugby Football Union would be barred from playing against the touring team.

Even if this was technically the end of the dispute, the Rugby Football Union did not forgive easily. When the Native team returned to London at the end of March, they were largely ignored by the Union and were given no official farewell from Britain.

However, one Union official must have occupied an ambiguous position. S. E. Sleigh, who had managed the New Zealand team to Australia in 1884, and made many of the advance arrangements for the Native team in Britain, had become a member of the Rugby Football Union committee during 1888. Regrettably, his views on the proceedings of the tour have not been recorded, although it may have been he who felt that the Union might have "given way".

Eyton included the following rather vague account of the international match in *Rugby Football Past and Present*.

NATIVE TEAM V. ENGLAND

England has maintained its supremacy in the football field. So much success has attended the New Zealand natives in their tour, that there were not a few supporters of our winter game who looked with some anxiety towards the trial of strength between the Mother Country and the Maoris. After the greatly improved form shown by the visitors, there was certainly a little reason for this misgiving, although the generality of the players seemed pretty confident. The result proved favourable for the Englishmen, who registered a goal and four tries to nothing. There was no doubt which was the better side, yet it must be admitted that an element of luck attended the Home sides early scoring. What struck one in the play, as much as anything, was the effective tackling of the visitors and the way they kept on the ball. Especially was this noticeable in the early period. Indeed, the first twenty minutes' play promised a brilliant match all through. A foolish mistake by W.

Warbrick, the full-back, gave the English the first try, and from this point the visitors seemed to lose heart. As the game subsequently progressed the back play of England became more and more brilliant, and the Maoris afterwards never appeared likely to win. Behind the scrummage the Home team had a great advantage. All the three-quarters ran and passed well, while Bonsor and Scott were both prominent at half. The latter, however, did more work than any of the backs, and from start to finish his play was always vigorous. Robinson, Cave, Evershed and Wilkinson were very prominent forward, and Royle proved safe at full-back. Forward, the Maoris were fast and kept well on the ball, while the pretty kicking of the backs at times elicited loud applause. Keogh took first honours in this respect. Some of the decisions of the officials caused much dissatisfaction amongst the Maoris, and early in the second half three members of the team withdrew from the field. This was caused in the following manner; Stoddart in running collided with the referee. His clothes had been torn just previously in such a manner as to necessitate his withdrawal. The players formed a ring around him, and he left the field to change. Then the visitors claimed to have a scrummage where Stoddart had run against the referee, but while they were protesting, Evershed got in, and the try was converted into a goal by Sutcliffe. After a few minutes' absence, the three malcontents were persuaded to return. This incident was greatly to be regretted, and more than one prominent unionist thought that the English might have given way. The match, however, proved exceptionally good, and the 12000 people present at the Rectory Field, in spite of the wretched weather and wet ground, seemed to thoroughly appreciate the play.

Bonsor kicked off towards the pavilion at ten minutes past three. Elliot failed to return the ball, but the forwards soon carried it to the centre. The play proved very fast in the first quarter of an hour, and there was really little to choose between the sides. Scott made several useful kicks and runs, but the Maoris showed superb defence, and each time repelled the attacks of their rivals. Free kicks for off-side were frequent, but they only served to relieve in turn the pressure at each end. Lockwood got away along the left side, after which there were a couple of pretty runs by Stoddart. For some time the play remained in the Maoris' quarters, and at length Bonsor dropped the ball behind the line. Warbrick — the full-back — attempted to run it out instead of touching down; and when half-time arrived the ball was close up to the English line.

The Maoris started the second period in dashing style, but brilliant play by the English forwards — in which Cave and Robinson were very prominent — got the ball to the other end. A beautiful pass from Sutcliffe to Stoddart enabled the latter to get a try after a brilliant run. His kick at goal failed. Then came the incident mentioned above, and Sutcliffe placed a goal from a try by Evershed, while subsequently another try was added by Sutcliffe. Next the Maoris had to touch down. In the last few minutes the New Zealanders came with great dash, and drove the ball over the line twice, but each time it was kicked against the boundary. Then "No-side" was called and England won by 1 goal and 4 tries to nil.[8]

The 1889 England team which defeated the Native team in controversial circumstances at Blackheath. Although it contained twelve new caps, ten of the team were experienced northern players. Timothy Auty

Why did the Rugby Football Union pursue an on-field dispute, serious though it was, to the length of demanding two apologies and threatening to end the tour? One answer is simply that they always regarded the game as being far more important than the individuals who played it. They stood by a strict code of sportsmanship and amateurism which demanded restraint and respect for the ideals of rugby and saw referees as being beyond question. On the other hand, from their earliest matches in Britain, the Native team had not conformed to these requirements. Their behaviour at Blackheath was not isolated, but merely the worst in a long list of indiscretions. A cynical view is that the Union needed a scapegoat through which to reaffirm its power and protect the reputation of its leading official, Rowland Hill. The idealism of the establishment was always under threat from pragmatists in the north, and more immediately from a British touring team which had failed to gain official sanction and yet still been heartily welcomed by rugby officialdom in Australasia.

The utterances of the sporting elite when the Native team arrived in Britain confirmed that games were a vitally important means of encouraging order in society and in the British Empire and of training imperial administrators. Team sport, especially, with its emphasis on group co-operation and loyalty, taught men the skills that would be necessary for much sterner challenges in business or on dangerous frontiers. The point of sport was not to win, but to participate, and to win or lose with equal dignity. The odds in life and in sport were that there would often be setbacks before eventual success. It was important to know how to cope with these setbacks and to persevere until success finally came. There was no disgrace in losing if one had done one's best.

This approach to sport was strictly amateur. But "amateur" meant more than hostility to professionalism and to the notion that individuals might use sport to earn money. It was also a code of conduct where one followed both the written rules and the spirit of the game. No advantage should be taken of an opponent which could not be reciprocated. As "gentlemen", who would not deliberately break the rules, players were expected to control their own behaviour without the intervention of a referee. Indeed, until the 1840s there were few appointed referees in public schools' football, the captains being left to resolve any disputes in an amicable fashion.

It is unlikely that many footballers took gentlemanly behaviour as seriously as the Corinthian Casuals — a team of ex-public school soccer players who withdrew their goal-keeper whenever a penalty was awarded against them. It was wrong, they claimed, to resist the consequences of a foul even when it was accidental. That a penalty existed for cheating did not make it acceptable to cheat at the risk of a penalty.

Men with similar public school backgrounds and views dominated the upper echelons of the Rugby Football Union. And during the 1880s, more than ever before, they saw a need to uphold amateur and gentlemanly codes of behaviour in sport. In both rugby and soccer, players in the north of England were becoming disturbingly competitive and showing signs that winning was more important to them than merely participating. Nowhere was this more apparent than in the ill-tempered reaction of the *Eton College Chronicle* in 1883 when Blackburn Olympic defeated Old Etonians to become the first northern team to win the FA Cup:

> Though it may seem strange that a football Eleven composed of mill-hands and working men should be able to sacrifice three weeks to train for one match, and to find the means to do so, yet when we reflect on the thousands who attend and watch the matches in Lancashire and so swell the revenues of the clubs, and on the enthusiasm of the employers of labour in the pursuits and successes of their countrymen, it is not a surprise.[9]

If gentlemen in soccer were disturbed by incipient professionalism, their counterparts in rugby were doubly concerned. The new International Board posed another threat, and the behaviour of the Native team probably confirmed fears that unhealthy influences were entering the game. A strong response to the visitors' behaviour at Blackheath was essential, and Rowland Hill ensured that it was made.

Since the beginning of the tour a close eye had been kept on the behaviour of the Native team, and initially they conformed to expectations. *The Times*, in its report of the Surrey match, said that it would not presume to congratulate the visitors for their conduct: it was exactly what was expected.

> We prefer ... to take it as a matter of course that they should have borne an equal part in the admirable discipline and self-repression exhibited in yesterdays [sic] contest, the instant and unquestioning obedience rendered to umpires and the total absence of those squabbles which once made a football match anything but an unmixed pleasure.[10]

Here was proof for all to see that the New Zealand players had learned well from the public school men who had introduced rugby to the colony during the 1870s.

From there, however, the situation had rapidly deteriorated. Against Kent and Moseley, reports suggested that the play of the Native team was rough; indeed Moseley justified their own rough play as a retaliation for "vicious methods" used against Kent. After further rough play in the Middlesex debacle, *The Field* said that several players should be severely lectured to, or left out of the team if they could not control their behaviour. In early November, *Punch* printed a mock report of a match under "Thugby Association" rules between "Midland Yahoos" and "North Country Savages", with an accompanying cartoon of John Bull declaring, "Play football by all means my boy — but don't let it be this brutal sort of thing".[11] While the Native team was not named, the skit and the cartoon coincided with complaints about it.

Three months later when the team returned to London and things went badly wrong for them against England, the press renewed their attack. One London correspondent to a northern paper showed no restraint:

> Saturday's match at Blackheath was entirely marred by the disreputable behaviour of the Maoris who conducted themselves in such a manner as to call forth the well merited censure of the spectators and everybody concerned. They not only disputed nearly every advantage gained by their opponents, but levelled abuse of the lowest type at the umpire and referee throughout the game ... Such an exhibition of rowdyism was never witnessed at Blackheath and the Rugby Union members present took no pains to conceal their disgust, while the spectators became irritated beyond measure at the unusual display of ill feeling in a match of this class.[12]

The Field mused that these events did nothing more than add to the existing reputation of the Native team for unsportsmanlike conduct. "[T]o leave the field simply because of an adverse decision is nearly the worst form that a football player can be guilty of."[13] Writing six years later, Frank Marshall praised the Native team for their play, but said they had marred it with "a most childish and unsportsmanlike display". Further, he felt that although the demand by the Union for an apology after the England international was distasteful, it was

Rowland Hill, controversial referee and stern critic of the Native team. He became secretary of the Rugby Football Union in 1882, and was still serving when New Zealand played England in 1925. Rugby Football Union

absolutely necessary. They had always maintained the highest principles of sportsmanship and respect for referees, and must continue to do so.[14]

Soon after the England international, *The Field* again attacked the Native team, this time for their play against London Welsh, suggesting that if others followed their example the reputation of rugby would suffer greatly. "[M]uch of the tackling was of a character to be decried ... on occasion the play became of an exceedingly rough and most undesirable description."[15] In sum, the New Zealanders were aggressive, over-competitive and antagonistic to match officials.

Yet this is only one side of the story. To search beyond London for criticism of the Native team is to search in vain. In the north of England the only press criticism was that written by London correspondents after the England international. Northerners had many more opportunities to watch and assess the play of the Native team, but they found nothing unusual to report. In fact, some found much to praise. As early as October the *Athletic News*, in Manchester, reminded its readers that an important distinction existed between "hard" and "rough" play. Eyton also commented favourably. "[T]he sporting press of

Manchester became almost members of the Maori brotherhood, and on the whole there was no need to complain that we were not fairly criticised."[16] Most encouraging of all was the report of the *Runcorn Guardian* after the first match against Widnes on 9 March.

> Whatever has been said ... [about] the conduct of these veterans of football, they are to be complimented upon the manner in which they acted at Widnes ... the universal opinion of spectators was to one effect — that they could not have seen fairer play shown by any team ... and the whole thing passed off with more tranquillity than usual.[17]

Two weeks later a return match was played.

The class structure of rugby in the north was completely different from that in the south. While the public school old boys had led the way in forming northern clubs during the 1860s, they were soon outnumbered there by small farmers, small businessmen, miners, factory workers and others who worked closely together in community and sporting affairs. These people were untouched by public-school traditions. Even the wealthiest northern rugby administrators had close contacts with working-class players. Although some of them had accumulated enough money to be considered part of the upper middle class, they were snubbed by its "gentlemen" who viewed hard-earned industrial wealth with a degree of contempt. More so than in the south, the northern elite maintained links with their local communities and with their working-class origins. They supported local clubs and mixed easily with working-class players.

A working-class game also meant greater tolerance of hard or rough play. Unlike gentlemen, and those in the professions, miners and factory workers were used to taking physical knocks as part of their daily routine. Taking them on the field was no different. It was almost inevitable that northern working-class rugby, and also Welsh rugby, became intensely competitive. Whereas the public school old boys supposedly played for character training, northerners used games between the various mining, mill and factory towns as a way of proving superiority and gaining status for their particular area. Strong community interest and support for the team meant that players had to practise and play, not just for their own enjoyment, but for the serious pursuit of victory.

This strong sense of competition was recognized with the introduction of the Yorkshire Challenge Cup in 1876. Within a decade this became the focal point of Yorkshire rugby, and cup ties attracted huge crowds who wanted to see exciting play as much as they wanted to see their community beating another. Not surprisingly, the Rugby Football Union strongly opposed cup rugby because, in their view, it placed too much emphasis on winning and not enough on the value of merely participating. It was also claimed that competition produced violence and dishonest methods in an effort to win. In 1882, soon after he had been appointed secretary of the Union, Rowland Hill wrote: "We believe that in some cases these matches have caused an evil spirit to arise, and that sometimes men are influenced more by the desire to win than to play the game in the true spirit."[18] In reality, Hill's view, like that of the *Eton Chronicle* in 1883, was as much a fear of professionalism as it was a case of regional snobbery and hostility. In the 1880s the respectable founders of rugby were having trouble coming to terms with the fact that large numbers of their players, and most of the best ones, were from different classes and backgrounds to their own.

It is easy, therefore, to understand why the Native team were accepted better in the north of England than in the south. Like the northerners they played a tough game, followed the letter rather than the spirit of the law and aimed to win rather than to lose with dignity. What some saw as roughness was easily accommodated within the ethos of northern rugby. Indeed if they had achieved their results with anything other than accepted methods, they would probably have been roundly criticized in the north. In the end the contrasting manner in which the team was treated in different parts of Britain perfectly reflected the wider divisions that were already showing themselves within British rugby. In 1895 these divisions split the game into two codes, one administered by the Rugby Football Union and the other controlled by the Northern Rugby Football Union.

The Rugby Football Union, and the public school old boys generally, could be forgiven for wondering where they had gone wrong with the Native team. For New Zealand rugby had originated among the old boys of English public schools. The first game in the colony, at Nelson in 1870, was largely organized by Charles Monro who had recently returned from Christ's College, Finchley.

This *Punch* cartoon accompanied a mock report of a "thugby" match (see page 89). If the comment on rough play was not aimed directly at the Native team, the coincidence is remarkable.

The following year rugby was organized in Dunedin by George Sale, the son of a Rugby School master, and he himself one of the original sixth formers who had penned "The Rules of Football as Played at Rugby School" in 1845. In Auckland, C.B. Mercer and C.G.R. Gore, old boys of Wellington College, England, converted the local clubs from Victorian to Rugby rules. Before long old boys of New Zealand schools such as Nelson College and Wellington College played their own part in spreading the game throughout the colony.

Instead of following the gentlemanly ideals and codes of conduct of these public school founders, however, New Zealand rugby players, and the Native team especially, quickly adopted the competitive spirit of the "anti-establishment" element in British rugby. There is no firmer statement of this than Tom Ellison's final recollections of Rowland Hill and the England international.

> As regards referees [sic] decisions, I am and I have always been, inclined to make large allowances for their frailties and to support them even to the length of conceding the commission of excusable mistakes, but this is surely the utmost limit that one can go. At any rate, I shall always consider myself entitled to raise my voice against any wrong decision by any referee, whoever he may be, that goes beyond the bounds of a reasonable or excusable mistake. For it would be asking too much of poor human nature to expect footballers to passively submit to all and any kind of decision that a referee may make, particularly when they are palpably wrong.[19]

Such forceful advocacy of the rights of players against referees may seem surprising from one who, when he wrote it, had played a leading role in the formation of the New Zealand Rugby Football Union. It was a strong and direct challenge to the Rugby Football Union and to the idea that referees were beyond criticism.

New Zealand rugby had become very similar to that in the north of England. Once the old boys had founded the game, they lacked the numbers to control it and impose their "higher traditions". As in the north of England, the men who played rugby in New Zealand were more likely to be farm labourers, miners and other manual workers, and the environments in which most of them worked produced the same tolerance for vigorous play. Many also lived in small isolated communities which began competitions with others once better communications made this possible.

In addition to these formative influences on the players in the Native team, the nature of the tour itself played a major part in shaping its methods and styles. Eyton and Scott needed them to keep winning to maintain public interest and profits. Consequently they always tried to put the strongest team into the field, and the players' approach to the game was likely to be uncompromising.

If the Native team did not come close to matching the expectations of the Rugby Football Union, there is ample evidence that the Union also failed to

The two umpires, Joe Warbrick and a Surrey official. *Illustrated London News*

practise the code it preached so loudly. The continuing dispute with Scotland and the International Board during the 1880s showed that the Union itself could also be uncompromising. The gentlemanly ability to resolve conflicts was not evident in that instance.

Speaking at a dinner after the Native team returned to Melbourne in May 1889, Joe Warbrick expressed doubts about the integrity of many English referees and match officials. Before the opening match against Surrey he had been warned by the touring Australian cricketers to expect difficulties in the interpretations of the laws by English referees. Furthermore, Warbrick said, although some of the behaviour of the British team in New Zealand had been regarded as objectionable, nobody else demanded the sort of apology that the Rugby Football Union had extracted from the Native team. Indeed, there were signs of another double standard in the Union's handling of the British tour of New Zealand. Although they had refused to sanction it, and had banned one of its players, they had no hesitation in selecting Andrew Stoddart for the international at Blackheath — after he had captained the British team for much of the Australasian tour.

In a country supposed to be the home of chivalry, Warbrick found much to fault in both opponents and spectators. "As long as they [the Native team] were losing they were jolly good fellows in the eyes of the crowd. But as soon as they commenced to win they were hooted and the papers were full of the weakness of the home side and the rough play of the visitors."[20]

The *Lyttelton Times* correspondent took a similar view of fickle English attitudes to rough play. Although a Maryport player had suffered a fractured jaw and a Blackheath player a fractured collar-bone, for the tourists "there is scarcely a member of their team who has not at one time been pretty seriously bent or broken. In fact, in Lancashire, Scott could not raise a sound fifteen".[21]

But such distinctions meant very little. It was the Rugby Football Union which controlled the game, and their view which mattered most. Rightly or wrongly, the conduct of the Native team was regarded as below standard and they were to pay the price when rugby historians, especially in Britain, came to pass judgement on the tour.

8
"*Quiet and well behaved*"?

Rowland Hill and the game at Blackheath provided the highest drama of the British tour, but the task of the Native team was far from complete. Despite the injuries, illnesses and controversies that still plagued the team, the last phase of the British tour was the most intense — twenty matches in only thirty-seven days. Yet the endurance of the team was such that they gained fourteen wins and a draw. Moreover, they established an undefeated sequence as remarkable as any in the annals of international rugby. In thirty-one matches in Britain, Australia and New Zealand, starting with their win over Widnes on 9 March and ending with their defeat of Wellington on 20 August 1889, the team won thirty and drew one. During the last three weeks in Britain only eight tries were conceded in ten matches.

Perhaps the team was sustained during this period by their experiences off the field. The longer they stayed in the north of England, the more hospitably they were treated. When the team left Britain at the end of March, their fondest memories were not of their victories but of people they had met. Their behaviour was not always perfect. Alcohol played a part in much of their misbehaviour, and in Belfast one player was arrested. As they did while playing football, the Native team off the field often tested the patience of those who were trying to clean up the image of rugby.

The six matches played immediately after the England international had mixed results for the team. Although they defeated London Welsh by two tries to one — in a match which *The Field* regarded as very rough and the Native team as very friendly — they then lost to both Oxford and Cambridge Universities. Eyton suggested that the Oxford result might have reflected the late festivities after the Cambridge game the day before. Next the team returned to Yorkshire and achieved easy victories over Manningham and Leeds before a surprise loss to Leigh on 27 February. On the strength of this performance, Leigh declared themselves equal to any club in England. It would be several years, though, before they consistently made their mark.

After scoring four tries in an untroubled victory at Runcorn on 2 March, the team's loss to Oldham two days later aroused controversy. According to Eyton, the game should never have been played as the ground was very hard

"A sudden outburst of joy on getting the 1st goal of the tour." *Illustrated London News*

and dangerous from frost. The Native team treated the surface cautiously and paid the price. Eyton also noted, not for the first time, that the opposition contained several leading players from other clubs.

    The following day the team bounced back with a four tries to nil success against Halifax who, in October, had inflicted one of the heaviest defeats of the tour, 4-13. Two days later, on 7 March, came defeat at the hands of Barrow and the end of an erratic three weeks which had produced four wins and four losses. A long rail journey on the morning of the Barrow match had left the Native team in low spirits and they lost to a rather weak team by a dropped goal to nil.

    On 9 March their remarkably long winning sequence began. Widnes, Manchester, Walkden, St Helens, Salford and Rochdale Hornets were overcome with little resistance. York came close on 20 March when the margin was only 4-3, and three days later Hull fought hard for a 1-1 draw in a return match, having won the first encounter 1-0 on 24 October. The return match against Widnes on 25 March, the last in the north of England, was as amicable as the first had been two weeks earlier. In an efficient 6-1 victory, Keogh scored two tries to take his tour total to thirty-four, easily ahead of Tabby Wynyard and Tom Ellison with twenty-three each.

OXFORD UNIVERSITY
RUGBY UNION FOOTBALL CLUB.

UNIVERSITY
VERSUS
MAORIS,
ON THE
MERTON GROUND,
On Tuesday, February 12th, 1889.

OXFORD UNIVERSITY, Selected from	MAORIS, Selected from
P. Christopherson, Univ., *Capt.*	J. Warbrick, *Capt.*
W. Rashleigh, B.N.C.	T. Ellison
C. J. N. Fleming, Queen's	C. Goldsmith
A. K. Lewis, Trinity	G. Wynyard
P. R. Clauss, Keble	W. Anderson
R. F. C. de Winton, Exeter	D. Gage
F. Morgan, Keble	W. Wynyard
W. E. Wilkinson, Keble	R. Maynard
F. Borwick, Trinity	*Ihimaira*
D. W. Evans, Jesus	P. Keogh
R. O. B. Lane, Trinity	*R. G. Taiaroa*
R. D. Budworth, Magd.	W. Elliot
N. F. Henderson, Magd.	E. McCausland
E. P. Simpson, Magd.	C. Madigan
J. E. Aldridge, Worc.	F. Warbrick
J. H. G. Wilson, Queen's	H. Lee
E. H. G. North, Keble	Alf. Warbrick
T. Parker, B.N.C.	*T. Rene*
R. S. Hunter, New	*W. Nehua*
W. T. Grenfell, Queen's	G. Williams
	D. Stewart
	Wi. Karauria
	A. Webster
	Arthur Warbrick

Kick off at 2.30 p.m.
Admission One Shilling.   Ladies Free.

Entrances, South Parks Road, and near Holywell Church, Oxford.

H. Beesley, Printer and Bookbinder, 4 Cowley Road.

The team card from the match against Oxford University on 20 February 1889. Ron Palenski

Almost inevitably, it seemed, these successes carried a price. For the match against Walkden on 13 March, seven leading players were injured. In the forwards, Sandy Webster reappeared for three matches after a long injury break, and Wi Karauria managed an appearance in spite of the tuberculosis which would claim his life before the end of the year. But the backs were severely restricted. Eventually Harry Lee, who had played forty matches in Britain as a forward, played ten more during the last month as either a centre or wing.

Arriving back in London on 26 March, the Native team found that little had changed in the minds of the Rugby Football Union and the sporting press. For a time the planned last match of the tour was in danger of cancellation as Surrey, Middlesex, London Scottish and United Hospitals all declined to provide opposition, although their reasons for doing so were not recorded. Eventually a Southern Counties team was assembled, though it was scarcely worthy of that designation as most of the players were drawn from the minor Essex and Sussex teams. The visitors even provided the referee, Joe Warbrick. In a very dull match, tries to Elliot, Gage and Fred Warbrick contributed to a 3-1 victory, the team's forty-ninth in Britain.

Immediately the *Lyttelton Times* correspondent attacked the Rugby Football Union for its handling of the match and the tour as a whole.

> The Rugby Union, I am ashamed to say, has allowed the New Zealanders to leave without offering them the faintest valedictory hospitality. The lack of courtesy with which the team has from first to last been treated in London has been scandalous.[1]

The Sportsman also felt sympathy for the team and pointed to a dramatic shift in attitude by the Union.

> [W]ithout wishing for one moment to defend the behaviour of certain of the players at Blackheath last month, some pity could not but be expressed that the farewell engagement of the dusky colonials should be brought off without the kindly countenance of the rugby governing body, who in the arrangement of the programme had at the outset done their level best to render the tour a success.[2]

On 30 March *The Field* published a lengthy and critical summary of the tour in which it said that the Native team had failed in all respects to match the expectations held for them.

> Their visit had been looked forward to with a good deal of pleasure. A report had certainly come forth that our dusky brothers were in the habit of playing a very rough game, but this was not altogether believed in. There was a greater tendency to hope, if not absolutely to believe, that the tour of the New Zealanders might do as much to benefit the popular winter game as the visits of the Australian cricketers had done for the national summer pastime. That this hope has been realised can scarcely be said; indeed we have heard no wish expressed that another team from the same quarter may soon be with us.[3]

The Field also said that public interest in the tour had been far less than that for many earlier cricket tours of Britain, a disparity accentuated when one remembered the much larger crowds which generally followed football in the north and Midlands. The reason for this lack of interest was directly related to the impression created by the Native team.

> The reason for this lack of more than ordinary interest will, we think, be found to rest with the players themselves. The conduct of some members of the team in several of the early matches proved the rumour had not lied. It was plainly shown that the education of these men had been obtained in a bad school. Their knowledge of all that is unfair surpassed their acquaintance with the legitimate game, and that is saying a great deal, for as a team the New Zealanders were an exceedingly good lot showing far superior form to what had been expected. The indulgence in these malpractices drew forth much unfavourable criticism, and also deterred many from attending the New Zealanders' matches who would otherwise have done so.[4]

Finally, and rather surprisingly in view of the few racial comments which had been made during the tour, the writer endorsed a suggestion by Scott that any future tour would be better without Maori players. "If by the elimination of that element, the objectionable features are removed, the team may anticipate a most hearty reception."[5]

In reply, Scott said he felt hurt at the attitude of the Rugby Football Union and the player boycott of the last match. A most abject apology had been given after the events at Blackheath and the past should therefore be forgotten. While he did not necessarily excuse the behaviour of some players, Scott insisted that their conduct had been very good in the majority of matches. He had letters to this effect from Oxford and Cambridge Universities and United Services, all major bastions of the gentlemanly ideal. Overall, when the heavy programme and extensive travelling were considered, Scott was pleased with the results of the tour and thanked the Rugby Football Union for their part in making it possible.

If the successes of the last six weeks in Britain had been soured by the return to London, the Native team retained many other fond memories as they departed for Australia. As Tom Ellison explained:

> Perhaps the most delightful part of our experiences were tasted not so much on the field as off it. On the voyage, landing at foreign ports, sightseeing, as guests of private people, football unions and clubs (although not many of them), large manufactuory proprietaries, and last but not least, of theatre managers.[6]

Eyton's tongue-in-cheek summary was in similar vein. "One would need to have graduated in New Zealand as a Minister of the Government of the present day to be proof against any ill effects from the numerous banquets offered us."[7] He said that unlike many footballers, the Native team had been welcomed whenever they returned to a previously visited hotel — although they had

THE RUGBY RUMPUS.

THE REV. MASTER T——: Oh, fie, go away naughty boy, I sha'n't play with boys who can't afford to take a holiday for football any day they like!

MASTER M——LL——R: Yes, that's just you to a T; you'd make it so that no lad, whose father wasn't a millionaire, could play at the game at all in a really good team. For my part I see no reason why the men who make the money shou'dn't have a share in the spending of it.

These caricatures are the Reverend Frank Marshall, official and historian of the Rugby Football Union and a terror to the professional tendencies of northern players, and James Miller, member for North Leeds on the Yorkshire Committee. *The Yorkshireman* sometimes made their own decision to change quarters because of the substandard food in certain establishments.

The hospitality was such that the team were forced to decline many invitations. Those they accepted were certainly diverse, including tours of cotton and woollen mills, glass factories, shipbuilding yards, a pen factory and the Guinness brewery in Dublin. Scott was able to obtain numerous free tickets to the theatre and music halls, as well as visits to areas generally not open to the public, such as St Thomas' Hospital, the Bank of England and Trinity College, Dublin. At other times the team attended athletics meetings, such as at Manchester where Eyton reported them as being unimpressed with the play of a touring American baseball team.

On several occasions Eyton rather cynically suggested that the best banquets and post-match receptions came from those clubs who had defeated the tourists. Yet Joe Warbrick had nothing but praise for his hosts.

> My impression of England and its people during the tour was a very favourable one, more especially does this apply to private individuals. I found them everywhere very kind and attentive and apparently anxious to make one's visit as pleasant as possible, never failing to show you anything that was of interest, historical or otherwise. This attention and thoughtfulness was apparent everywhere I went and created in me no little surprise as I had often heard that the English people were noted for their exclusiveness.[8]

The singling out of "private individuals" was undoubtedly a reference to the London press and the Rugby Football Union. Not surprisingly, Eyton's recollection of the best receptions during the tour referred almost entirely to northern and Welsh clubs. Apart from Cambridge University and the Scottish club Hawick, he noted Stockton-on-Tees, Hartlepool, Cumberland, Wigan, Llanelli, Bradford, Warrington and Widnes. Pie Wynyard also had pleasant memories of his time in Manchester and Ireland and of Christmas in Wales.

In the end not even this amount of goodwill could compensate for the strains of the tour on the field. David Gage, among others, said that the team had enjoyed the trip and had been well received, but the fatigue and anxiety caused by the itinerary had removed much of the polish. When Eyton wrote his tour book in 1894, he suggested a different sort of fatigue.

> Speechifying became monotonous. The referee was invariably the best we had met with, the local team were the best players and the nicest fellows, the umpires did their duty most effectively, the captains of both teams were splendid fellows, and so on repeated at each place visited. The songs were good, bad and indifferent.[9]

In early November Scott had also complained that he was tired of the social obligations of speeches and football dinners.

"Quiet and well behaved"?

As injuries mounted, the team were inclined to spend most of their non-playing days playing cards or billiards, prompting Bully Williams to a positive recollection of his team mates. "Socially, they were quiet and well behaved, and would have shown a good example to Europeans in their general conduct on and off the field."[10]

Williams' recollection should not be taken lightly. In the late nineteenth century, sporting administrators, and especially those in rugby, were determined to establish strict control over players' behaviour off the field as well as on it. If sport was to serve an educational and moral purpose, and rugby was to counter accusations of barbarism, it was important to curb traditional elements such as drinking, swearing and gambling. The earliest constitution of the New Zealand Rugby Football Union included disciplinary clauses to discourage these activities, as well as "lavish expenditure on the entertainment of teams". In 1897 the Taranaki union suggested that the New Zealand captain needed to be "a steady man and one who will be able to keep the men well in hand in order that the prestige of New Zealand, as regards behaviour as well as skill, may be retained".[11]

With similar views prevailing during the late 1880s, Joe Warbrick had been quick to offer a reassuring prediction for the Native team. Before their departure from Napier in June 1888, he had insisted that

> ... whatever they did on the field, they would do nothing off it unworthy of representatives of New Zealand, and ... the charges levelled against some teams who had visited the old country should not be levelled against the Native footballers.[12]

Warbrick was presumably referring to the behaviour of Australian cricket teams in England.

Others in New Zealand had promised an equally smooth path for the Native team, especially in the matter of alcohol. Writing in the London *Daily Chronicle* at least a month before the team arrived in Britain, a Mr Hilton declared that they would be "abstainers" as they were bound by an agreement not to take "strong drink". A group of New Zealand gentlemen had apparently written to Hilton asking that he, through the press, discourage British people from offering the team alcohol. Eyton made no mention of these arrangements.

Whether Hilton's concern was simply to do with rugby players, or the wider issue of "native" people consuming alcohol is uncertain. Twenty years earlier Australian humanitarians had launched a bitter attack on the promoters of the Aboriginal cricket tour, accusing them of sordid exploitation and saying that the players would be vulnerable to all kinds of excesses. It was claimed that alcohol contributed to the declining health of many Aboriginal team members on a preliminary tour of Victoria and New South Wales in 1866, and to the eventual deaths of two of them. Although, when the Aboriginal team reached Britain, the problem never reached the proportions that many had feared, one player was arrested for assaulting two policemen while drunk, and there is evidence that another had a serious drinking problem. Right to the end of that tour the Central Board for the Protection of Aborigines remained critical of the arrangements.

By comparison, the drinking "problem" of the Native team caused little concern, and the perception of the team as something other than vulnerable "natives" tended to divert attention away from the alcohol issue. Nevertheless, there is ample evidence that the team indulged themselves in ways that later touring teams did, even if these ways were not approved by the rugby establishment. Most blatant was what happened at the Middlesex match when, after having drunk champagne at lunch, the team's performance was affected and two players were found sleeping in a shrubbery. Six weeks later a potentially more serious incident occurred after a banquet in Belfast. A member of the team, not named by Eyton, became involved in an altercation on the wharf and was promptly arrested. Attempts by the team management to gain his release were met by abuse from the player — clearly suggesting drunkenness — and he was left to cool off overnight in a cell. Eventually, after the intervention of a police inspector who was also a member of the local rugby union, he was released with only a light penalty.

Alcohol also played a part in the loss to Oxford University on 20 February. As Eyton noted, "Festivities at Cambridge the night before had not done our boys much good; as Oxford University, though not an extra strong team, managed to win".[13] And after a particularly hospitable reception in Birmingham, the *Lyttelton Times* correspondent referred to the matter as follows:

> All day long too over-hospitable citizens were inviting them to "liquor-up". Indeed, how to avoid the constant lushing without giving offence has so far been one of the most difficult problems the New Zealanders have had to face.[14]

It was popularly understood that Bill Elliot earned his nickname "Mother" precisely because of his efforts to control those members of the Native team who had gone astray in these situations.

Such behaviour is hardly surprising in a touring team, and there is no reason to believe that these were the only indiscretions. What is surprising is the frankness with which Eyton described them. Writing in 1894, only two years after the New Zealand union had put its strict constitution in place, he did not hesitate to report either the Middlesex incident or that in Belfast. Nor did he shy away from discussing the potential for a controversy about drinking by Maori.

As the differing interpretations of sportsmanship on the tour had revealed, off-field conduct was not yet under the firm control of the rugby unions. Throughout the 1890s, and as late as 1905, the New Zealand Union was struggling to curb gambling, bad language and rough play, especially that of a Wellington provincial team in 1897 who were dubbed "the butchers". (Reports in the press also suggested problems about the behaviour of players.) But in New Zealand and Britain, reports of the Middlesex match and references to "constant lushing" raised not the slightest ripple. That Eyton even mentioned these incidents in his tour book, is proof enough that he saw little harm in doing so. He simply reflected a public, but not public *school*, acceptance of the realities of rugby. While the official civilizing process had managed to curb the violent excesses of the 1870s, it had not yet adopted the somewhat puritanical expectations about the behaviour of later All Black teams.

If members of the Native team were guilty of indiscretions, so were many others. The British rugby authorities singled out the tourists for attention, but their view was clearly not shared by the wider public and by players. For a later generation to highlight sensational aspects of their behaviour, both on and off the field, and to allow this to obscure the memory of their playing record, is an injustice which takes no account of the environment in which the Native team moved.

The departure of the team from Britain at the end of March 1889 was accompanied by mixed feelings. While the London press was unrelenting in its criticism, most of England, Ireland and Wales had made the tourists very welcome. There were also contrasting views among the Native team players themselves. Pie Wynyard, who had gone to England on his own business and played fewer than a fifth of the tour games, enjoyed the whole experience.

> The trip home is a dream of every footballer, and my impressions of the tour of the Native team will never be effaced from my memory. I am unable to express sufficiently the pleasures experienced. The voyage, the sights seen, the hospitality and kindness experienced in Britain are tremendous items to write about.[15]

Joe Warbrick, although contributing little as a player, but nevertheless at the heart of proceedings, was more critical.

> As a country England did not quite come up to my expectations, and this is a prevalent opinion of New Zealanders and perhaps is due to the fact that from infancy we read and hear of nothing else but England, and the imagination gets imbued with perhaps extravagant notions. That it is a wonderful country there are no two opinions ... but as a place of amusement England is, I should say, the rich man's paradise and the poor man's Hades.[16]

This seems a more accurate summary of the feelings of the team than Wynyard's. But whichever recollection is closest to the mark, statistics make their own statement about the Native team's performance in Britain.

From 3 October 1888 to 27 March 1889 they played seventy-four matches in six months for forty-nine wins, five draws and twenty losses. Clearly the Native team had thoroughly mastered the playing standards of their time.

Tom Ellison. Player, captain, tactician and expert administrator, he lead the New Zealand team to Australia in 1893, devised wing forward play and the 2-3-2 scrum, and wrote *The Art of Rugby Football*. Rugby Museum, Palmerston North

Still there was a suggestion from Tom Ellison that they could have, and should have, done better. His final verdict on the style and strength of British rugby was hardly encouraging to the home of the game.

> I was not very largely impressed with the play of the Britishers; for, with all of the players they had available, I saw no one to compare with Jack Taiaroa, J. Warbrick, Whiteside, Keogh & co, except Lockwood, Stoddart, Valentine, Bonsor and a very few others. Their play generally was of the one style and description from start to finish — hooking, heeling out and passing all day long whether successful at it or not. I never played against a team which made a radical change of tactics during the course of a game. They all seemed to have tumbled into a groove and stuck there. They were generally big strong fellows, but they never struck me as being clever players.[17]

Although the team was leaving Britain, the tour was far from its end. On 29 March Scott and most of the touring party left Plymouth for Australia to play both Victorian Rules and rugby matches. On 5 April Eyton and Pie Wynyard followed them. Before the team disbanded, another five months would elapse, and more controversies would ensue.

9
"Playing stiff"

The Australian leg of the tour is little more than a testimony to the motives of Scott and Eyton as speculators. With the exception of some matches in New South Wales, and the representative fixtures in Queensland, the standard of rugby was not high. Indeed, a number of minor matches against eighteen-a-side teams, and those under Victorian and Association rules, were, at best, festival exhibitions. Their purpose was simply to make money and it hardly mattered that the Native team were unpractised and unfamiliar with local codes. But as in Britain, it is clear that Scott and Eyton overestimated their market and the crowd-pulling power of the team.

Australia also provided its share of controversy. In Brisbane the team was again beset by accusations of professionalism and disreputable playing conduct, which resulted in the suspension of four players, much unwanted publicity and a formal enquiry. The damage caused by these events was much greater than the actual issues involved. At tour's end the team could point to a superb playing record and widespread support for most of their actions. Yet to the rugby hierarchy and the press, Australia revealed more of the dubious behaviour and breaches of conduct that had marked the departure of the team from New Zealand. For many of the team's critics there seemed little reason to change the opinions that they had formed a year earlier.

In Britain in mid-November, when the injury toll was at its most severe, a number of leading players had vowed that they would not undertake the Australian leg of the tour. A letter to *The Press*, received after the team arrived in Australia, said that the players were tired of football and had little enthusiasm for the Victorian game. In the end, however, threats to quit did not amount to anything. Four players, Gage, Ihimaira, Webster and Karauria, did return to New Zealand without playing in Australia, but all had valid reasons for doing so.

When he arrived at Lyttelton in May 1889 David Gage said that he was returning home because of a sick relative. He had no animosity towards the Native team and reappeared in five further matches when they returned to New Zealand. For the other three players it was a matter of injury or illness, and none of them reappeared in New Zealand. Smiler Ihimaira, described by Eyton as constantly unfit, played only fourteen matches in Britain and was invalided home. Karauria missed only five matches during the first four months in Britain, but then became almost constantly ill and died of tuberculosis within months of his return. Sandy Webster, who played in all but two of the first thirty-seven matches in Britain, played in only three thereafter.

Three more players, McCausland, Anderson and Stewart, left the team after its matches in Victoria, and their motives for departing are less certain. It is likely that McCausland had employment obligations. He had taken only twelve months' leave from his bank job in Auckland, and this was due to expire at the end of June 1889. Nothing is recorded of Anderson and Stewart except that they reappeared in the final tour match against Auckland on 24 August. But the real consequence of these departures, especially McCausland and the durable Gage, was to reduce the strength of the team to only nineteen for the matches in New South Wales and Queensland. An even greater burden was placed on those who remained.

In the eyes of Scott and Eyton, Australia was a promising environment to tour. The warm climate and colonial prosperity provided an ideal base for the expansion of sport. With the creation of a uniquely Victorian football code by Thomas Wills and others during the late 1850s, the pattern of local rivalries and lucrative spectator interest was set in place. In New South Wales and Queensland rugby emerged as the preferred game, and the first match between these two colonies attracted great public interest when it was staged in 1882.

However, the Native team's venture into the Victorian game was a failure in every respect. The hectic schedule in Britain had left Jack Lawlor no opportunity to fulfil his role as coach. Consequently the team which took the field for the first Victorian Rules encounter against Maryborough on 15 May 1889 knew little about the rules of the game or its basic skills. It was comprehensively beaten 1/2 to 6/9, which under present scoring values would have been 8-63. Three days later there was a slight improvement as the team lost to Ballarat 0/4 to 4/2 (4-26), but the substantial 2/4 to 13/16 (16-94) loss to Carlton on 25 May proved that the Native team stood little chance against leading Melbourne clubs.

> The play, though at times laughable, was not exciting, and Carlton were able to take matters easily right through. Mr Traitt, who was field umpire, made the matter as easy as possible for the Maoris by considerably shutting his eyes to their errors which, however, were less frequent than might have been supposed.[1]

According to Tom Ellison, the major difficulty facing them was a lack of specialist back players to compete with Victorian teams in such an open game.

Although Lawlor and several local players assisted the Native team, their only wins under Victorian rules were achieved against the comparatively weak Wanderers, South Melbourne and Daylesford sides. St Kilda, 6/7 to 1/6 (49-12), and Essendon, 11/4 to 5/5 (70-35), inflicted heavy defeats. More importantly,

"Playing stiff"

Members of the Native team in Queensland. By this stage at least seven members of the original touring party had returned to New Zealand, and four more were to be suspended following the match against Queensland. Bill Brien Collection

none of these matches attracted a significant number of paying spectators, and their only contribution to the tour was to add to the high physical toll that it had already exacted.

On the rugby field fortunes were much better. In their first match against Melbourne RFC on 24 May, the Native team scored five tries to two to win 13-6. For reasons unknown, the match commenced at 11 am and was followed by lunch. The next outing was something of a festival affair against a Navy XVIII drawn mostly from officers of HMS *Orlando* and HMS *Calliope*. In the spirit of the occasion the Native team reversed their usual formation: forwards played as backs and backs played as forwards. Nevertheless the usual backs, Madigan, Keogh, Fred Warbrick and Tabby Wynyard scored most of the points in another 13-6 win. It was here that Wiri Nehua contributed one of his three tour tries from eighteen matches, and Anderson one of his two from fifty-eight. Rather surprisingly, the biggest win in Victoria was the 19-0 score against the full Victorian team on 11 June, which included one try each to Keogh, Ellison and Maynard, and two to Fred Warbrick.

Having travelled to Sydney, the team faced New South Wales on 15 June and won an even match 12-9 in front of 10,000 spectators.* This result was followed by an easy 17-7 defeat of Sydney University and a 21-0 romp in a festive match against a Parramatta Club and King's School XVIII. The return match against New South Wales at the Sydney Cricket Ground on 22 June produced another close encounter which the Native team won 16-12. The final matches in Sydney, against Arfoma and a Permanent Artillery XVIII, produced emphatic 27-3 and 32-10 victories. In the first match Goldsmith, who had scored only one try from twenty matches in Britain, achieved a hat-trick. In the second, Madigan and Ellison also secured three each as the Native team ran in ten tries, a total which was exceeded only in the match against Canterbury on 17 August. True to form, only one of these tries was converted, and this by Dick Maynard who landed only five goals during the whole tour. The Arfoma match also left three of the local players with broken ribs.

Leaving Sydney at the end of June, the team played soccer matches against Northumberland at Maitland and Newcastle at Newcastle. Both resulted in heavy defeats for the Natives, 3-6 and 2-6 respectively. Apart from these, the journey north to Queensland was a leisurely one and the team did not take the field again until 15 July.

Amid much pageantry, and in front of 8,000 spectators, the first match against Queensland was a very one-sided affair — eight tries to the Native team as they won 22-0.** For once on the tour the local press made no excuses. They acknowledged that the Queensland team was one of the strongest that had represented the colony, including among its talented players Charles Speakman, who had settled in Australia after touring with the British team during the previous year. Yet Queensland stood no chance.

> The combined play of the visitors simply nonplussed the local men. Their passing was like machinery, the Queensland forwards never seeing the ball after it came out of the scrummage, and the backs were not strong enough to stop the "clockwork" of the visitors ... The visitors had Maori passwords indicating the locality of the ball in the scrummages, which puzzled the local men.[2]

Two days later a Toowoomba XVI were despatched 16-0 and an Ipswich XVIII surrendered 17-5 on 19 July. By then the Native team had an undefeated record in rugby matches on Australian soil, having won twelve in succession.

Unfortunately, this very success was to count against them as serious

---

* In New South Wales, tries counted three points, conversions two points and dropped goals four points. So it was noted that under the scoring values used in New Zealand, where all goals were worth more than a try, the result would have been a 6-4 win to the home side.

** In Queensland, tries counted two points, conversions three, and dropped goals four.

"Playing stiff"

accusations surfaced during the return match against Queensland on 20 July. Throughout the first half a number of spectators were greatly surprised by the very poor play of the visitors. Only exceptional efforts by Billy Warbrick, at fullback, ensured that the scores remained close. As the *Brisbane Courier* observed:

> Some of the Maoris seemed scarcely up to form in the early part of the game, but towards the end they all appeared to work exceedingly well ... The best man of the team, W. Warbrick, upheld his reputation well.[3]

Eventually, with two tries to Elliot and one each to Fred Warbrick and Williams, the Native team regained its composure to win 11-7. But the damage had already been done.

Immediately there were claims that members of the team had been bribed to "throw" the game so that others could take advantage of the long odds for a Queensland victory being offered by local bookmakers. According to one Brisbane report, the full-back, presumably Billy Warbrick, had been offered £50 if "he would let the local men go past him occasionally".[4] Eyton and another local reporter both suggested that the transformation of play by the Native team during the second half had only followed strong words by Joe Warbrick at half-time and his threat to reveal the names of players and bookmakers involved. As Eyton recalled:

> It was on the occasion of this match that four of our players were thought, in racing parlance, to be playing "stiff", and that they had been got at by some bookies; at all events, when accused of it at half-time and cautioned, they played a different game in the second half ... There is no reason why this match should not have been won almost as easily as the first, though perhaps Queensland had improved a bit.[5]

Eyton made no further comment, and the press also contained no other details of the allegations or the terms involved.

The immediate outcome, however, was the suspension by Scott and Eyton of four players — Goldsmith, Keogh, Madigan and Arthur Warbrick — pending further investigations. Thus the touring party was reduced to a bare fifteen for its last Australian match against a Toowoomba XVII on 22 July. And for the first time in over a year of touring, a replacement player was accepted by the Native team: Charles Speakman, who scored one of five tries in a 19-0 victory. So ended the Australian tour — fourteen victories in succession, but the matter of the suspensions still not settled.

The Northern Rugby Union of Queensland saw no need to take any action over the strange events at Brisbane, and no correspondence from them was ever forthcoming. Predictably perhaps, the New Zealand provincial unions took a much stronger line than Queensland had. When the team reached Invercargill in early August, the Otago Union despatched a strong telegram to Eyton.

Charles Speakman, member of the 1888 British team and one of only two substitute players used by the Native team. He played for them against Toowoomba after the touring party had been severely depleted by defections and suspensions.
Timothy Auty

Billy Warbrick, fearless and incorruptible fullback. Reportedly offered £50 to "let the local men go past him occasionally", he instead played brilliantly against Queensland and saved the Native team from a potentially greater fate.
Thomas Eyton, *Rugby Football Past and Present*

> Statements to public papers here and elsewhere re four men ... suspended for shady practices in Brisbane have never been contradicted. The Otago Rugby Football Union declines to play or sanction any match in which these men take part until a public contradiction of that statement has been made and a most ample and satisfactory explanation of the circumstances which gave rise to it is given to this union.[6]

It seems that the first priority of the Union was to secure a public denial. The truth would come later.

At a dinner following the Southland match on 7 August, Eyton expressed confidence that he could prove to the Otago Union that there was no truth to the allegations. In a letter to that body a few days later he insisted that the four players had been suspended only to allow a proper investigation to take place. Indeed, a recent team meeting had called for their reinstatement on the grounds that there were serious doubts about the case against them.

Charges of gambling meant more than a threat to the future of amateur rugby. Many people in New Zealand viewed gambling as a vice on the scale of drinking and prostitution. It was seen to threaten the vital ethic of hard work and saving, and to entice men away from a settled responsible life. The 1881

Gaming and Lotteries Act prohibited most forms of gambling in New Zealand, and most of what remained was channelled through horse racing. Even there strenuous efforts were made to control off-course betting. In short, if any truth was found in the charges against the Native team, the response would doubtless have been as vigorous as anything previously mustered by the Rugby Football Union.

No details are known of the inquiry held by the Otago Union when the team reached Dunedin. However, one player admitted that during the tour he had taken a bet on the result of the England international — for a new hat! The outcome of the inquiry was an official resolution dismissing all charges. But again the Union's main concern seemed to be that the rumours had not been denied, regardless of their validity.

> [H]aving heard all the available evidence regarding charges against certain members of the Native team, and having received an explicit denial from the accused members, and satisfactory explanations from the management, the committee is of opinion that there are no facts before them justifying the accusations against these members of having sold the match at Brisbane on 20th July, and that the committee regrets that the rumours which emanated from the Native team itself were not promptly contradicted by the management.[7]

Bearing in mind the hostility of Otago towards the Native team before the tour, especially concerning the addition of Pakeha players, it is a safe assumption that the final decision in favour of the team was not arrived at lightly. The outcome was generally welcomed by the public and press. Only the Southland Union was not fully satisfied, feeling that there was strong evidence to proceed with charges against at least one player.

This was not the first time that the Native team had been involved in financial intrigues. A year earlier their departure from New Zealand had been marked by numerous allegations of professionalism and speculation. Moreover, there is a familiar note concerning some of the players who were suspended. During the final weeks in Britain, both Keogh and Madigan were in dispute with Scott over money and they refused to play in one game at Manchester. Finally, in 1891, Keogh was banned from rugby by the Otago Union on charges of professionalism, specifically for gambling on the results of matches in which he was playing.

With these clouds hanging over them, and the diminishing number of fit players, the return of the Native team to New Zealand had not proceeded at all smoothly. But on the field, and for all to see, they had a few more opportunities to redeem their reputation.

10
Much more than a circus

With four players under suspension and an injury to Pie Wynyard sustained in Queensland, the Native team was reduced to fourteen fit players when it returned to New Zealand on 5 August 1889. The numbers declined even further when Harry Lee was injured during the match against Southland two days later. A replacement player, W. Hirst, the Southland full-back, was pressed into service for the match against a Mataura District XVI at Gore. Yet morale was high and the confidence of the Native team knew no bounds after their winning exploits in Australia. As *The Press* reported, "They are unanimous in describing their New Zealand matches 'soft things' and say that the English team which visited the colonies last season would not be in the same street as them".[1]

The first match back in New Zealand, at Invercargill on 7 August, attracted 2,000 spectators on a fine afternoon. Although playing only fourteen men, and thirteen after the retirement of Lee during the second half, the tourists scored three tries to one in a comfortable victory. The next day, with Hirst at full-back, but still only fourteen men, they ran in six tries against Mataura District. For once on tour the goal-kicking was also up to standard, Ellison landing four conversions and Nehua one.

With playing stocks restored after the Otago enquiry into the Brisbane affair, the team were now able to present to the New Zealand public a brand of combined rugby far removed from that of the previous year. In an exciting match against a typically strong Otago side, they scored five tries to two and were only threatened on the scoreboard by two dropped goals from Downes. This marked the end of the tour for Keogh, who stayed in Dunedin when the team moved to Christchurch.

Finding that Hawke's Bay were also on tour when they reached Christchurch, Scott was quick to arrange a match at Lancaster Park. Public interest was such that the Mayor requested a 2 pm shop closure so that employees could see the game. By all accounts the Native team did not play with great dedication or seriousness, but the result was a display of running rugby which produced nine tries in a 13-2 scoreline. Goldsmith secured another hat-trick and Alf Warbrick, who played only sixteen matches in total, collected two of his four tour tries. *The Press* was extravagant in its praise of the play, comparing it with the quality of the British touring team during the previous season.

It is within the bounds of possibility that no New Zealand team could successfully cope with the Maoris in their present improved form. Combination was a big feature in the game, and the wearers of the black passed with remarkable accuracy and quickness between their legs, over their shoulders, under their arms and with their feet. Their collaring was also good, In fact their play must have reminded the spectators of that fine exhibition of football we received from the English team when it was here.[2]

Two days later Canterbury were treated to even greater punishment. Although the match was refereed by Rev. John Hoatson, the Canterbury team selector, this was of no assistance to the locals. Hoatson was regarded as a very sound referee, but a somewhat erratic selector. Eyton noted that for some reason the Native team were especially determined to "win all they knew" against Canterbury, and the plan was executed with eleven tries, but only two conversions, as they won 15-0. Gage and Elliot scored three each, and the *Lyttelton Times* was most impressed. "The Natives were evidently more on the job than they were on Thursday against Hawke's Bay, and the local team proved nothing more than a chopping block upon which the 'Blacks' exercised their abilities."[3]

The account of the match in *The Press* was also full of praise for the tourists.

NATIVE TEAM V. CANTERBURY

The reappearance of the Maori team against a team representing Canterbury drew together on Saturday afternoon a large crowd of spectators to Lancaster Park where the match was played. On Friday night and early on Saturday, rain fell heavily, but during the match the weather was fine and the ground in far better condition than many expected to find it. Great interest was shown in the match. It was generally conceded beforehand that Canterbury would be vanquished, and it was acknowledged afterwards that our picked fifteen fought against greater odds than they ever did, the English representatives alone excepted. The play showed [sic] on Saturday afternoon was a fine exhibition of what several months of combination and practice will do. When last here the Maoris it was plainly evident had a lot to learn. They have learnt it, picking up and noticing those little apparently insignificant details taken together, have a marked effect in the result of a football contest. That they can play offside is palpable, but apart from this, it must be admitted that they were far and away too good for our local men. In the loose, in the scrum, dribbling, passing, collaring and running, they were very much indeed Canterbury's superior. Such runs as were made by W. Warbrick at full-back, by Madigan, Gage and W. Wynyard, the passing of H. Wynyard, F. Warbrick and all the backs, as well as several forwards, the rushes of Alf Warbrick, Maynard, Taare, Taiaroa and Rene, and the dodging and fending powers of nearly every one, non plussed their opponents, who failed even to score as many points as Hawkes Bay did against the visitors. Of the Canterbury team, everything cannot be said in their praise. They commenced well with the wind in their favour, but they were soon overpowered, a result partly brought about by the poor play of some of the backs. Ward and McLean were not brilliant, and the later [sic] did less than the former; Creswell from some cause failed in his usual effective kicks, and the passing among them was only of second rate character. Donnelly and Hobbs were just the opposite, running, collaring and kicking well, and Wilson again earned his position at full-back. But what, comparatively, was the good of any of them? Throughout the second spell the visitors appeared to simply play with them, and the many good rushes of our forwards were stopped by a Maori very smartly picking up at their feet and passing to a "confrere" who sent the leather on, and in less time than it takes to say it, the play was again at the old spot — mostly on the Red's side of the centre-flag. Notwithstanding that the match was considerably one sided, the result reached was anticipated, the public seemed well satisfied with the afternoon's exhibition of football, and if at times disapprobation of the Maoris play was shown, any good run and clever pass, or some pretty dribbling or feinting never failed to receive a hearty cheer. The Canterbury men, who were beaten by 15 points to 0, were continually cheered on, but cheering was no good against the combination, strength, condition and science of the visitors.[4]

Journeying to Masterton, the team met a surprisingly strong Wairarapa combination on 19 August, but won 10-8, Ellison and Gage scoring all of the points. Arriving in Wellington the next morning, the tourists went directly to their match against the provincial team and won it 4-1. Wellington's only try was scored by Syd Nicholls, the father of three All Blacks of the 1920s. Yet Eyton did not have fond memories of the occasion. "This match was not a pleasant nor interesting one, and the number of deadheads on the ground was equal to the best records of Wellington's openhandedness."[5]

It was intended that the next opponent would be Taranaki at New Plymouth, but the length of the stop by the Wellington-Auckland steamer was not enough to allow this. With the touring party again reduced to a bare fifteen, and all of them tired from the hectic schedule, Eyton did not regret the omission.

On the field the team were dramatically redeeming themselves, and public interest in the tour increased rapidly. However, the party which reached Auckland for the final tour match on 24 August had lost several key members. Lee had left with injury after the Southland match, Keogh had remained in Dunedin and Gage and Ellison in Wellington. Nehua and Sherry Wynyard had also departed on the journey north, and apparently Joe Warbrick was again carrying an injury, not having played since Gore. Eyton recalled that the team was also weakened in the same way they had been prior to the match against Oxford University: "... extra festivities occasioned by a reunion with some of our boys' Auckland friends were not conducive to a good game on the morrow".[6] Thus, in spite of a great deal of public support and predictions generally in favour of the Native team, Auckland were able to repeat their

Patrick Keogh, "the artful dodger". Thomas Eyton, *Rugby Football Past and Present*

success of the previous year, winning 7-2. Each team scored two tries, but Auckland added a dropped goal and a conversion; thus they became the only New Zealand provincial side to have played and been undefeated by the Native team.

Off the field a familiar pattern had unfolded between the team and the provincial unions. Southland had displayed its hostility by wanting to continue with an enquiry into the Brisbane affair even after charges had been quashed. Otago, although it had responded positively by dismissing the charges, then annoyed Scott by offering a very low forty percent of gate receipts against his demand for sixty per cent. Eventually, when the Union realised there would be extreme public disappointment if a match was not played, they agreed to split the gate fifty-fifty.

For the match against Hawke's Bay in Christchurch, the dispute concerned jurisdiction. The Hawke's Bay Union said that it would only sanction a match against the Native team if it was played in Napier. The Hawke's Bay team replied that as it contained all of the senior club captains and a majority of delegates to the Union, the match should be recognized — as it duly was.

Arrangements with the Canterbury Union appear to have proceeded without incident. But an editorial in *The Press* launched a stinging attack on the team for their behaviour during the match and on the tour as a whole.

> [C]ertain of their number distinguished themselves by the most discreditable language, some of it directed personally to one of the umpires and the referee. We can hardly imagine that they learned this from playing with English teams, and must regard it as an accomplishment which they have initiated on their own account. It is one that can well be dispensed with, and we trust that the respectable members of the team — for we give them credit for having some such among their number — will for their own credit take the matter up. If not, they will find that the public will be disposed to afford but scant encouragement to Native teams in the future...[7]

In Wellington, negotiations with the Union became very delicate. First, Scott informed the Wellington secretary that unless he could secure the Basin Reserve, with its obvious potential for a large gate, the team would not play in the capital. The Union replied that it was unlikely that the Wellington City Council would agree to Scott's request, but that a match could be arranged for Newtown Park with the visitors receiving seventy-five percent of the gate. Apparently not even this was acceptable to Scott, and on the morning of the match it was reported that public demand for a fixture had forced the Wellington Union to offer all gate receipts, less expenses, for a game at Newtown Park.

The match against Auckland was placed in jeopardy when Scott demanded sixty percent of gate against a Union offer of fifty per cent. Again the promoter had his way. Having failed to make money in Victoria, and having drawn only a meagre return from Britain, Scott saw the New Zealand games as the last opportunity to turn a worthwhile profit. Whether this eventuated is not known. But the Wellington match, especially, shows that Scott and Eyton were able to use the lever of public demand to force the hand of the provincial unions towards their terms.

The unions were far from blameless in these disputes. Their general offer of a fifty percent gate, and particularly Otago's forty per cent, was considerably less than standard practice during the tour of Britain, and also less than the sixty percent offered to both the British and the Native team during the previous year. Naturally the unions wanted to gain their own advantage from what was becoming a popular public spectacle. But it is a fair indication of their collective attitude to the Native team that they sought arrangements lower than established precedent.

The feeling of the unions at the end of the tour was also evident in their attitude to several proposals which emerged for another tour in the near future. As early as October 1888, a Mr Pratt of Christchurch had discussed taking a second Maori team to Britain and North America. His plans, which were said to involve members of the Taiaroa and Ellison families, soon collapsed. In April 1889, when private interests in Wellington announced plans for a fully

The 1892 Wellington representative team — including Harry Lee, Tom Ellison and Sherry Wynyard. Irwin Hunter, *Rugby Football: Some Hints and Criticisms*

representative New Zealand team to tour Britain, condemnation was swift. The Otago Union said that constant touring would lead to professionalism, and any future tour must be under the authority of the New Zealand unions. Nelson and Auckland issued similar statements, and Canterbury, while happy with the idea of a tour, also insisted that it must be under union control. It was four years before another team left New Zealand: this was for a tour to Australia in 1893 under the auspices of the recently formed New Zealand Rugby Football Union. Indeed, it seems that the formation of this body in 1892 owed a good deal to the problems caused by the Native team and its private backers. Only those who conformed to the standards of the Union, on and off the field, would be allowed to carry the New Zealand game abroad.

Comparing teams from different periods is almost impossible to do impartially. Perhaps the most sensible and least controversial approach is to try to determine how well a team was able to dominate the top standards of its time. Using this approach to compare the Native team with both the 1905 and the 1924 All Blacks, the Natives can claim high honours, perhaps even higher than either of their more famous successors.

Arthur Swan, New Zealand's greatest rugby historian, has suggested that fewer than half of the games played by the Native team in Britain would be designated first class by modern standards. In the highest grade he included the three international matches, and also all of the English county sides and the leading Welsh clubs. But if Swan's analysis is technically true, it is also deceptive. Supposedly representative county sides such as Northamptonshire, Cumberland County and Devonshire were in no way superior to many of the northern club sides which Swan deemed not to be first class. But it is the northern clubs which are crucial to the comparison with the All Blacks of 1905 and 1924. Only the Native team — and neither of the two All Black teams — can claim to have encountered the full weight of British rugby strength during the period in which they played. The split of British rugby which led to the formation of the Northern Union in 1895 left the traditional union game but a shadow of its former self during the first quarter of the twentieth century. In terms of cold statistics the consequences for rugby union were disastrous.

In 1893 the Rugby Football Union had affiliated to it 481 clubs including more than 150 in Yorkshire and a large number in Lancashire. By 1903 defections to the Northern Union had reduced this number to 244 clubs, and the original numerical strength was not regained until 1925. At its 1898 annual general meeting the Lancashire County Rugby Union could claim only eight affiliated clubs, and in 1901 Yorkshire had only fourteen. Moreover, after winning seven of the first eight county championships up to 1895, Yorkshire did not regain the title until 1926, and Lancashire not until 1935.

As for England teams, after dominating international competition during the 1870s and 1880s, they became extremely weak. Not once in the eighteen years between 1892 and 1910 did they win the Triple Crown, the symbol of rugby supremacy in the British Isles. Match statistics for England's internationals tell the story in stark fashion: in 55 games from 1871 to 1895 England won 35, drew 11, lost 9; in 52 games from 1896 to 1910 they won 16, drew 5, lost 31. This reduction in the strength of the Rugby Football Union supports the view that teams opposing the 1905 All Blacks were on the whole much weaker than those of seventeen years earlier. In 1888-89 the Native team played at least forty of their seventy-four matches against clubs who subsequently joined the Northern Union or against teams drawn from such clubs. Included in this were nineteen of the twenty-two clubs involved in the original 1895 breakaway. Another telling point about the northern split is that the England team which took the field at Blackheath in 1889 contained eight Yorkshiremen and two Lancastrians.

By contrast, of the thirty-two matches that the 1905 All Blacks played, only four were against northern clubs, and in these the tourists scored 150 points while conceding only three. Included was a 40-0 defeat of Yorkshire. Not surprisingly the England team which lost 15-0 to the All Blacks at Crystal Palace contained only two northern players, both from Durham City, far from the former heartland of northern rugby. Indeed, at the end of the 1905 tour *The Field* put matters into perspective when it suggested that the success of the All Blacks was as much due to their own considerable skills as to the lack of combination from the many "scratch" teams fielded against them. Only the Welsh clubs had been well drilled and "homogeneous" in their approach. Yet Welsh rugby was also much weaker than previously. Many Welshmen had defected to the Northern Union game — so many, in fact, that the new code was soon able to organize international fixtures between teams designated "England" and "Wales".

For the tour of the "Invincibles" of 1924 a similar, if less extreme, pattern can be found. Only five of their twenty-eight matches in Britain were against northern teams. Of these, Northumberland and Lancashire performed the best, but only in losing to the All Blacks by twenty-three point margins. Although Yorkshire won the county championship in the following season, it made no contribution to the England team that played the All Blacks, the single northern player being from Liverpool.

It is true, of course, that the two famous All Black teams lost only one match between them whereas the Native team lost twenty. But the circumstances in which these results were achieved were markedly different. Playing no more than thirty-two matches, neither of the All Black teams faced even half of the fixture list of the Native team in Britain — to say nothing of the latter's matches in Australia and New Zealand. In 1905 the 32 matches were spread over 109 days, approximately one every 3.5 days. In 1924 the 28 matches occupied 112 days, one every 4 days. The Native team, however, played 74 matches in 175 days, one every 2.3 days.

Even without these comparisons, both the Native team players and contemporary observers of them were quite aware of the magnitude of their performance. George Williams, for one, was pessimistic about the chances for future touring teams in Britain.

> I have been so often asked whether (in my opinion) a strictly speaking representative team of New Zealand could sally forth on such a tour as that of the Native team and return with higher honours? I answer emphatically no. It might be, if limited to 30 or 40 matches, they would put down Yorkshire, All-England, Middlesex and such teams as inflicted the heaviest defeats upon us, but this is even then improbable.[8]

Joe Warbrick reinforced this with a scathing reference to the performance of the 1893 New Zealand team in Australia.

> What may I ask would be the fate of the last New Zealand team that journeyed to Australia if they had been asked to play three matches a week in the same time (6 months) when with 23 and a reinforcement of four more they attributed their defeat at the end of a fortnight to staleness ... I certainly do not think they would defeat an All-England team. A Rep. team that can be defeated by New South Wales twenty-five points to three would certainly have small hopes of coping successfully against the flower of English football. Neither do I think that any New Zealand team would be equal to the best 15 of the Native team when they returned in 1889, all being fit and well.[9]

Forerunners of the All Blacks

A Warbrick family group during the early 1890s, Fred, Ella, Joe, Lucy. Rugby Museum, Palmerston North

Ironically, this 1893 New Zealand team was captained by Tom Ellison, a strong critic of British playing methods in 1889.

Assessments from the Native team management were mixed. Scott, whose objectives always lay beyond the field, told *The Sporting Life* that prospects for a future tour were excellent. "We have much better talent than was included in the present combination and if able to obtain anything like a representative side, could doubtless secure a still better record." [10] Eyton was more encouraging. "Eventually ... the ugly duckling throve exceedingly and became — I have no hesitation in saying — the best and handsomest exponents (as a touring team) of rugby football in any part of the world."[11]

George Dixon, who managed the 1905 All Blacks, was another to praise the Native team. He pointed to the scepticism that had accompanied their departure, and suggested that at that time they were little better than an average provincial side. By the end of the tour, however, they had developed a combination and record to surprise even their strongest critics. Irwin Hunter, a leading Otago player of the 1880s who became a noted writer on the game, also disputed any suggestion that the Native team were not of the highest standard.

> When the Maoris came back at their full strength, no team in New Zealand could have looked them in the face ... The Maori team was not strong when it went away, but what made that team was the picking up of Keogh and the great capacity for observation and imitation possessed by the Maoris ... I think the football they showed was the best we have ever seen in this country.[12]

Conclusion

Why has the Native team not assumed a more honoured place in the history of New Zealand sport? And why did it fade from the national consciousness after the high praise given to its play in 1889?

The rugby establishment, both at "home" and in New Zealand, was not hostile to the team at the beginning of its tour. Having gained the standard guarantees of its amateur status, the Rugby Football Union had no problem in extending their patronage to Warbrick's proposal early in 1888. The New Zealand unions agreed to play the team and to support it with a share of gate money. They even implied that their jurisdiction did not extend to Maori players, and they took an interest only when Pakehas were added.

As soon as the team took the field, however, this initial support was sorely tested. The financial objectives of the promoters, accusations of professionalism and questionable playing methods produced suspicion and antagonism. If the New Zealand unions could not bring themselves to try to prevent the tour, nor did they encourage it.

In Britain these issues continued to simmer and finally boiled over at Blackheath. It did not seem to matter that the wrong-doings of the Native team were no different from those of many northern and Welsh players, or that players in these areas found no fault with the team. All three groups — Natives, northerners and Welsh — fell foul of a "gentlemanly" rugby authority which stood its ground and clung to public school ideals. In 1888-89 the Native team provided a convenient scapegoat for various tensions in rugby between the north and the south of England, and it was seventeen years before another New Zealand team toured Britain. As W.J.T. Collins wrote in his *Rugby Recollections*, "It is probable that the long interval between the visit of the Maoris in 1888-89 and the All Blacks in 1905 was partly due to the suspicion that there were malpractices on the part of the Maoris, as there were by lots of English and Welsh clubs on tour".[1] Nor, despite the intervening First World War, does the nineteen-year gap before the next All Black tour in 1924 compare favourably with that between the first two Springbok tours in 1906 and 1912.

At the end of the tour, the Brisbane affair and Scott's "money-grubbing" approach to the New Zealand unions revived memories of the previous year. While the public loudly praised the new brilliance of the Native team's play, officialdom had little reason to believe that anything important had changed. In this stance they were as hypocritical as the Rugby Football Union.

In an effort to boost the New Zealand game, the provincial unions had readily stood out against the parent body in England and welcomed the privately organized and speculative British tour of 1888 — one with a taint of professionalism far stronger than that associated with the Native team. To criticize the Native team at the end of their tour, while continuing to ignore the questions hanging over the British, reveals a very selective interpretation of control and interest that was clearly not based on the higher ideals of rugby.

The Native tour showed that there was a significant gap between the public image claimed by administrators and the private reality pursued by players. Rough play, rougher language and high-spirited behaviour off the field has always been common in rugby. The Native team were boisterous, perhaps loutish at times. But they were not unusual in their behaviour, and they were no more deserving of criticism than any other team. Perhaps the problem was that on the field they chose openly to question what they saw as unjust, and that off it they failed to keep their behaviour away from the public eye. The role model that New Zealand rugby should have had from its first touring team to Britain was instead sabotaged by a self-interested double standard based on a pursuit of power by the provincial unions.

What of the wider significance of the tour to New Zealand? Certainly the Native team was not a fully representative colonial selection, and perhaps the predominantly Maori composition had less public appeal than was expected. But having more than adequately proved that they could hold their own with the Mother Country, thereby implying that all colonial stock was up to standard, perhaps they were entitled to more formal recognition than they got. They were, however, essentially a private venture. By 1905 there was a single rugby authority for New Zealand, and perhaps more importantly, the country had a more highly developed national consciousness. Even more than most of the Prime Ministers who succeeded him, Richard Seddon saw the political capital to be gained by virtually conferring ambassadorial status on an All Black team. Indeed, the final stages of the 1905 tour, through British Colombia and the United States, were financed by the New Zealand Government as a public relations exercise.

Memories of the Native team have faded badly, and with that their reputation has suffered. Much rugby writing of recent times has treated the team less than seriously. Obviously there is a problem with finding detail beyond Eyton's rather selective account of the tour. But the tendency has been to highlight only the sensational aspects — the Middlesex champagne incident, the England international, the Brisbane affair and various anecdotes of dubious accuracy. Writers such as Winston McCarthy, Gordon Slatter, W.M. Reyburn and Keith Quinn have variously suggested that many of the team played in bare feet throughout a British winter, and that the spirit of the tour was such that the team were unhappy to disband.[2] The massive itinerary, which shaped almost all aspects of the tour, is frequently discussed in terms of disbelief and doubt about the quality of most of the opposition. While the celebrated Deans "try" against Wales in 1905 has become part of rugby folklore on both sides of the world, few are aware of the circumstances of the controversy which dogged the Native team before and after the England international.

Emphasizing indiscretions and the unusual creates an impression that it was the Native team who were at fault. The real successes of the tour, such as the victory against Ireland and numerous others against strong opposition, are lost in accounts which tell more about an exotic, barnstorming circus than about a talented and committed touring team.

The heroes of the 1888-89 Native team are not those who organized, promoted and financed the huge enterprise, but the twenty-six players whose resilience ultimately made it possible. After the great toll of injuries and illnesses, and the many hardships and tensions, what was the long-term effect of the tour on team members? Pat Keogh felt that the itinerary in Britain contributed directly to the early deaths of many: at least ten were dead by 1904 and all but seven by 1926. However, four of these deaths were due to accidents, one to typhoid and others to causes that seem unrelated to the exertions of rugby. In fact, of the eight players who appeared more than fifty times in Britain, only Ellison who died at 36 and Gage who died at 48 failed to live to the age of fifty. The next youngest to die was George Williams, at 69.

If the tour did not exact its price physically, there are signs that it left a bitter legacy in the minds of some players. Keogh may have been wrong in his facts, but his opinion is revealing in itself. Similar dark views appear in Tabby Wynyard's obituary written in 1938, fifty years after the tour.

> The Natives suffered severe hardship and a continual shortage of clothing and luxuries, even food, owing to the fact that the "gates" in Britain were generally very poor, a few coppers only being charged for admission to the games. They were often compelled to reside (unlike our modern spoon-fed rugby teams) at third rate boarding houses and hotels, and on several occasions arrived at snow-clad railway stations at midnight with nobody to welcome them and had no option but to sleep on the benches there.[3]

This is a rather extreme summary of the tour, but one perhaps derived from the recollections of a player who did not have entirely fond memories of his experiences.

If the tour produced unhappy memories for some in the Native team, later many of them still made positive contributions to New Zealand rugby. Seventeen of them appeared in provincial teams in the five years following the tour, and,

Conclusion

perhaps surprisingly, two gained the ultimate respectability of captaining New Zealand. Tom Ellison ended his representative career by leading the team to Australia in 1893, and David Gage finished his international career by captaining New Zealand against Queensland in 1896. Bill Elliot was given the Auckland captaincy, and George Williams and Tabby Wynyard, in particular, lingered as respectable elder statesmen of the New Zealand game. Only Pat Keogh went down the path that most critics of the Native team had feared, and even he was pardoned by the Otago Union in 1895.

Far from being a blot on the landscape of sport in New Zealand and Britain, the Native team deserves a position of honour. It was the first New Zealand sports team to tour Britain, and the first international rugby team to tour there from any part of the world. In its time the team was treated seriously by friends and foes alike. Some of the reactions to the tour now seem quaint and disproportionate, and the players' exploits almost unbelievable. This only indicates the passing of time and changing expectations. It does not justify the widespread ignorance about the Native team's achievements.

Notes

Except for specific points of clarification, most of these references are to direct quotations. A full set of references to all aspects of the New Zealand Native team is contained in my MA thesis, "'The Originals'; The 1888-89 New Zealand Native Football team in Britain, Australia and New Zealand", University of Canterbury, 1992.

CHAPTER ONE

1. R.H. Chester & N.A.C. McMillan, *The Encyclopedia of New Zealand Rugby*, Auckland 1981, p.206; I. Hunter, *Rugby Football: Some Hints and Criticisms*, Auckland 1929, p.10.
2. *Canterbury Times*, 17 February 1888, p.15.
3. *The Sporting Life*, 27 September 1888, p.4.
4. T. Eyton, *Rugby Football Past and Present*, Palmerston North 1896, p.5; Chester & McMillan, p.280.
5. Eyton, pp.5-6.
6. R. Holt, *Sport and the British*, Oxford 1989, pp.83-6.
7. R.T. Kohere, *Autobiography of a Maori*, Wellington 1951, p.65.
8. A. Shrewsbury, letters to Mr Turner, 15 May/3 June 1888. Letter Book — photocopy in possession of R.H. Chester, Auckland. Shrewsbury expressed his own regret at not making an offer to Warbrick while in New Zealand.
9. *Canterbury Times*, 16 March 1888, p.16.
10. *New Zealand Parliamentary Debates*, 1888, Vol.63, p.155.

CHAPTER TWO

1. Unless specifically stated, biographical details for team members are mostly derived from Chester & McMillan, *Encyclopedia*; A.C. Swan, *History of New Zealand Rugby Football 1870-1945*, Wellington 1948, pp.519-26, and "Makers of History: The 1888-89 N.Z. Native team", *Silver Fern*, 1,8,15,22 July 1965.
2. Eyton, pp.9-15.
3. The names Taare Koropiti and Charles Goldsmith are both used in match reports throughout the tour. Goldsmith is preferred here, as it was that which was entered on his death certificate, Gisborne, July 1893.
4. McCausland obituary, unknown source, Auckland 1936; Elliot interview, *The Press*, 11 April 1954, p.16.
5. McCausland obituary; death certificate, P. Keogh, 12 March 1940. A further possibility that George Williams was born in England is not confirmed by his death certificate which records his place of birth as Auckland; death certificate, G. Williams, 27 April 1925.

Notes

CHAPTER THREE

1. *The Weekly Press*, 8 June 1888, p.697.
2. *The Press*, 25 June 1888, p.6.
3. *Lyttelton Times*, 21 July 1888, p.3.
4. *The Press*, 9 July 1888, p.5.
5. *Ibid*, 16 May 1888, p.5.
6. *The New Zealand Referee*, 9 March 1888, p.188.
7. J.O.C. Phillips, *A Man's Country?*, Auckland 1987, p.95.
8. *The New Zealand Referee*, 22 June 1888, p.54.
9. *The Weekly Press*, 29 June 1888, p.816; *The New Zealand Referee*, 6 July 1888, p.79.
10. *The New Zealand Referee*, 6 July 1888, p.79; 20 July 1888, p.78; *The Press*. 18 July 1888, p.6.
11. Shrewsbury, letters 15 May; 3 June 1888.
12. *The New Zealand Referee*, 23 November 1888, p.9.
13. *Canterbury Times*, 1 June 1888, p.15.
14. R. Gate, *Rugby League: An Illustrated History*, London 1989, p.19; F. Marshall, *Football: The Rugby Union Game*, London 1894, p.504.
15. *Canterbury Times*, 22 June 1888, p.14.
16. *Otago Witness*, 20 July 1888, p.26.
17. *The Weekly Press*, 27 July 1888, p.976; *The New Zealand Referee*, 10 August 1888, p.140.
18. *The New Zealand Referee*, 20 July 1888, p.98.
19. *Otago Witness*, 3 August 1888, p.26; *The New Zealand Referee*, 20 July 1888, p.98.
20. *The Press*, 12 July 1888, p.5.
21. *The Press*, 1 August 1888, p.5.
22. *The Weekly Press*, 27 July 1888, p.75.
23. *The Press*, 1 August 1888, p.5.

CHAPTER FOUR

1. Eyton, p.6.
2. *The Sportsman*, 28 September 1888, p.4; *The Daily Telegraph*, 28 September 1888, p.8.
3. *Illustrated London News*, 13 October 1888, p.418.
4. *The Press*, 13 November 1888, p.5.
5. Eyton, p.18.
6. *Ibid*, p.19.
7. *Lyttelton Times*, 19 December 1888, p.2.
8. Eyton, p.19
9. *Lyttelton Times*, 19 December 1888, p.2.
10. Eyton, pp.19-22.
11. Quoted in K.S. Inglis, "Imperial Cricket: Test matches between Australia and England 1877-1900", in R. Cashman and M. McKernan, eds, *Sport in History*, St Lucia 1979, p.149.
12. *The Daily Telegraph*, 28 September 1888, p.8.
13. *The Times*, 4 October 1888, p.8.
14. C. Bolt, *Victorian Attitudes to Race*, London 1971, pp.6-7.
15. *The Field*, 6 October 1888, p.505; *Illustrated London News*, 13 October 1888, p.418; *The Daily Telegraph*, 4 October 1888, p.8; Williams in Eyton, p.91.
16. *The Times*, 4 October 1888, p.8; *Hawick Press*, 27 November 1888 in Eyton, p.27.
17. *Dewsbury Reporter*, 3 November 1888, p.2.
18. Eyton, p.17; *The Sporting Life*, 4 October 1888, p.4; Marshall, p.505.

19. *Lyttelton Times*, 22 November 1888, p.3.
20. *The Rochdale Times*, 20 March 1889, p.7.
21. *The Times*, 4 October 1888, p.8; *The Field*, 6 October 1888, p.505; *The Sportsman*, 4 October 1888, p.4.
22. Eyton, p.72.

CHAPTER FIVE

1. Gate, p.16.
2. Eyton, p.24.
3. *Ibid*, pp.24–5.
4. *Hawick Press* 27 November 1888, Eyton, p.27.
5. Eyton, p.29.
6. A. Pullin, *Alfred Shaw: his career and performances,* London 1902, p.101.
7. *Lyttelton Times*, 7 March 1889, p.2.
8. *The Press*, 6 March 1889, p.2; *Lyttelton Times*, 5 June 1889, p.2.

CHAPTER SIX

1. Quoted by J.J. Stewart, *Creative Rugby*, Petone 1979, p.40.
2. Eyton, p.23.
3. *Lyttelton Times*, 24 February 1889, p.2; Warbrick in Eyton, p.112.
4. *Lyttelton Times*, 8 January 1889, p.2.
5. Eyton, p.76.
6. *Lyttelton Times*, 12 February 1889, p.2.
7. Eyton, p.49.
8. *Lyttelton Times*, 26 February 1889, p.2.
9. Eyton, p.81.
10. *Lyttelton Times*, 10 April 1889, p.2
11. Eyton, p.82. The italics are mine.
12. Warbrick, *Ibid*, p.112.
13. Eyton, pp.31-5.
14. *Ibid*, p.35; *The Press*, 24 January 1889, p.5.
15. Eyton, p.41.
16. *The Press*, 11 February 1889, p.6.
17. Eyton, pp.41–4.
18. *The Field*, 6 October 1888, p.505; 15 December 1888, p.880; *The Illustrated Sporting and Dramatic News*, 13 October 1888, p.125; 19 January 1889, p.515.
19. *The Daily Telegraph,* 4 October 1888, p.8.

CHAPTER SEVEN

1. Eyton, p.47.
2. *Ibid*, p.52.
3. *Ibid*, pp.53,54.
4. *Ibid*, p.57.
5. T. Ellison, *The Art of Rugby Football*, Wellington 1902, p.68.
6. *Ibid*.

Notes

7. *The Press*, 11 April 1889, p.2.
8. Eyton, pp.61-3.
9. C. Andrew, "1883 Cup Final; 'patricians v. plebeians'", *History Today*, (33) May 1983, p.25.
10. *The Times*, 4 October 1888, p.9.
11. *The Press*, 13 December 1888, p.6.
12. *Bradford Observer*, 23 February 1889, p.5. This was a northern paper, but the writer was a Londoner.
13. *The Field*, 23 February 1889, p.272.
14. Marshall, *Football*, p.506.
15. *The Field*, 23 February 1889, p.272.
16. Eyton, p.77.
17. *Runcorn Guardian*, 13 March 1889, p.8.
18. E. Dunning and K. Sheard, *Barbarians, Gentlemen and Players: A Sociological Study of the Development of Rugby Football*, Canberra 1979, p.156.
19. Ellison, p.69.
20. *The Press*, 6 June 1889, p.5.
21. *Lyttelton Times*, 16 April 1889, p.3.

CHAPTER EIGHT

1. *Lyttelton Times*, 4 June 1889, p.3.
2. *The Sportsman*, 28 March 1889, p.4.
3. *The Field*, 30 March 1889, p.451.
4. *Ibid*.
5. *Ibid*.
6. Ellison, pp.64-5.
7. Eyton, p.73.
8. Warbrick, *Ibid*, p.111.
9. *Ibid*, p.73.
10. Williams, *Ibid*, pp.91-2.
11. Swan, p.126; Phillips, p.126.
12. *Lyttelton Times*, 21 July 1888, p.3.
13. Eyton, p.64.
14. *Lyttelton Times*, 19 December 1888, p.2.
15. Pie Wynyard in Eyton, p.115.
16. Warbrick, *Ibid*, p.111.
17. Ellison, pp.65-6.

CHAPTER NINE

1. *The Press*, 6 June 1889, p.2.
2. Eyton, p.85.
3. Quoted in P.A. Horton, "A History of Rugby Union Football in Queensland, 1882-1891", unpub. PhD thesis, University of Queensland 1989, p.415.
4. *Otago Witness*, 8 August 1889, p.27.
5. Eyton, p.85.
6. *Otago Witness*, 8 August 1889, p.27.
7. *The Press*, 10 August 1889, p.5.

CHAPTER TEN

1. *The Press*, 16 June 1889, p.2
2. *Ibid,,* 16 August 1889, p.6.
3. Eyton, p.86.
4. *Press.* 19 August 1889, p.3.
5. Eyton, p.87.
6. *Ibid.*
7. *The Press,* 19 August 1889, p.2.
8. Williams, *Ibid,* pp.91-2.
9. Warbrick, *Ibid,* p.112.
10. *The Sporting Life,* 28 March 1889, p.4.
11. Eyton, p.6.
12. Hunter, p.7.

CONCLUSION

1. W.J.T. Collins, R*ugby Recollections,* Newport 1948, p.126.
2. See W. McCarthy, *Haka: The Maori Rugby Story*; K. Quinn, *The Encyclopedia of World Rugby*; W.M. Reyburn, *A History of Rugby*; G. Slatter, *On the Ball.*
3. W.T. Wynyard, obituary 1938, newspaper cutting, unknown source.

Appendix 1
The players

Few details are known about most of the players. Eyton offers little of substance, even failing to provide full names of some. A number of them played no representative rugby outside the tour and thus became forgotten men. Another problem is that birth and death registrations for Maori were often inaccurate or non-existent during the late nineteenth century. Identification was also made difficult by the departure of a number of the team to Australia during the 1890s.

ANDERSON, W.? (? -c.1893) Forward.
A number of sources mention that Anderson was also known as Keri Keri, and he may therefore be the W. Keri Keri on the Te Aute College roll in 1882-83. Selected for the tour from the Hokianga club, he played at least 48 matches in Britain and was described by Eyton as "the hardest grafter in the team; always on the ball and did a tremendous lot of useful work, quiet and unassuming". Returning to New Zealand before the end of the Australian tour, Anderson played no other representative rugby and died in the Hokianga area shortly before Eyton wrote his tour book in 1894.

ELLIOT, William (1867-1958) Half-back.
Bill "Mother" Elliot was an Auckland representative in twenty matches from 1887 to 1896, including several as captain. One of the five Pakeha players in the Native team, he appeared at least 63 times in Britain and emerged as one of the leading players of the tour. Selected for Tom Ellison's 1893 New Zealand team to Australia, he was subsequently unable to tour.

Although he worked for a time in the New Zealand Railways workshop at Wanganui, he spent most of his life in Auckland. Elliot was the last survivor of the Native team, outliving Dick Taiaroa by almost four years.

ELLISON, Thomas Rangiwahia (1867-1904) Forward.
Both on and off the field Ellison's life was one of considerable achievement. A cousin of Dick Taiaroa, he was born at Otakou on the Otago Peninsula and educated at the Otakou Native School and Te Aute College. A Wellington representative on 23 occasions between 1885 and 1892, he ended his rugby career as captain of the New Zealand team to Australia in 1893. On the Native

tour he played at least 58 matches in Britain and 25 in Australia and New Zealand, winning high praise from Eyton for his performances. " [As] a forward ... [he] was second to none in the Native team. His knowledge of the finer points of the game, his weight, strength and activity rendered his services invaluable."

A provincial referee, Wellington selector and member of the management committee of the Wellington Union at various times throughout the 1890s, Ellison's contribution to the foundation of the New Zealand Rugby Football Union was crucial. It was on his motion that New Zealand adopted a black uniform with a silver fern as its official playing colours. His book, T*he Art of Rugby Football,* remains a classic work on early rugby strategy. In it he outlines the principles of wing-forward play and the 2-3-2 scrum formation which characterized New Zealand rugby until the early 1930s.

Widely believed to be the first Maori to enter the legal profession, Ellison studied law in the Wellington office of Brandon & Hislop and was admitted to the bar in 1891. On three occasions he was an unsuccessful parliamentary candidate for Southern Maori, and in 1901 he petitioned parliament for consideration of Ngai Tahu land claims.

GAGE, David Richmond (1868-1916) Three-quarter.
Educated at Waiomatatini primary school, St John's and St Stephen's Native Schools, Gage obtained a Makarini scholarship to Te Aute College in 1882. Making his provincial rugby debut for Wellington in 1887, he also represented Auckland and Hawke's Bay in a playing career that lasted until 1901. Such durability was much in evidence on the Native tour where Gage took the field in 68 of the 74 matches in Britain and thirteen in New Zealand. He did not take part in the tour of Australia because he had a sick relative in New Zealand. Between 1893 and 1896 he appeared eight times for New Zealand and captained the team in his last match against Queensland.

Gage worked as a Maori interpreter throughout the North Island and was later employed by the Wellington City Council. When he died, leaving a wife and six children, the Poneke Rugby Club raised a significant sum of money to pay for a memorial stone and to support his family.

GOLDSMITH, Charles (Taare Koropiti) (c.1869-1893) Three-quarter.
Selected for the Native team while still a student at Te Aute College, Goldsmith played only twenty matches in Britain. He was, however, good enough to make five appearances for Hawkes Bay in 1889 and 1890. He died in Gisborne Hospital from lung complications.

IHIMAIRA, E. ("Smiler") (? — ?) Forward.
Although regarded as one of the characters of the Native team, little can be

Appendix 1: The players

traced of Ihimaira's life beyond it. Eyton described him as " The Don Juan of the team ... very strong but not extra fast. Was somewhat of the old 'bullocking' style of player, but came off occasionally". Selected for the Native team from Te Aute College, Ihimaira was frequently unfit or injured and made only fourteen appearances in Britain. Finishing his representative rugby career with three matches for Hawke's Bay in 1891, he was reported to be working as a publican in Hawke's Bay in 1925.

KARAURIA, Wi (? -1889) Forward.
Selected for the tour without any provincial record, Karauria soon proved his worth. Eyton considered him "an excellent forward player [who] was generally liked". He appeared in forty-two of the first forty-eight British matches, including thirty-two in succession. He then suffered from tuberculosis. Sent back to New Zealand before the Australian tour, he died shortly afterwards.

KEOGH, Patrick (c.1867-1940) Half-back.
The leading try scorer and star player of the Native team on the field, Keogh was seldom shy of controversy off it. One of the Pakeha players, he was born in Birmingham, England, and arrived in New Zealand about 1871. Educated at the Christian Brothers School, Dunedin, he played for the Kaikorai club from 1884 and Otago from 1887. In Britain he appeared 60 times and scored 34 tries.

Long remembered as one of the brilliant backs of early Otago rugby, Keogh's career came to an abrupt end in 1891. After inept play for Kaikorai against Alhambra, he was accused of having money on the result of the game. Although denying the charge, he admitted taking bets during the previous season, and retired before the Otago Union could hear his case. In due course the union declared Keogh a professional and disqualified him. However, in 1895 an application for reinstatement was successful, although he did not play again.

Keogh worked as a brass moulder in Dunedin, but his later life was marked by mental illness and numerous convictions for drunkenness. He was reportedly given six months' hard labour for assaulting his wife in 1905, and he spent much of the period from 1913 to 1940 in Seacliff Mental Hospital where he died of bronchial pneumonia.

LEE, Harry (? — ?) Forward.
In spite of reports that Lee was seriously injured early in the 1888 season, and even that he had contracted scarlet fever, he was in Napier for the start of the tour and appeared at least 50 times in Britain. He played once for Southland in 1887 and once for Wellington in 1889, and ended his representative career with three matches for the latter province in 1892. A stalwart of the Poneke club, nothing else is known of his later life, although Keogh suggested that he was dead by 1926.

MADIGAN, Charles (1866-1896) Three-quarter.
A Pakeha player, and an Auckland representative in nine matches from 1886 to 1890, Madigan appeared only thirty-two times in Britain. Very fast and one of the best defensive backs in the Native team, he suffered numerous injuries, including a broken ankle against East Cumberland. Frequently described as being in bad health during the 1890s, and as dangerously ill in 1893, Madigan died in Auckland from lung complications.

MAYNARD, Richard (c.1866-1897) Forward.
Maynard was regarded by Eyton as a "very strong and determined forward player, one of our very best and always ready for the field". A regular player in Auckland prior to the tour, he appeared in at least thirty-eight matches in Britain, despite injuries, and seven times for Auckland in 1889 and 1892. Moving to a farm near Gisborne, he played for Poverty Bay in 1894, but died of typhoid three years later.

McCAUSLAND, Edward Elsmere Montgomery (Mac) (1865-1936) Three-quarter and full-back.
Born at Sandhurst, Victoria, McCausland came to New Zealand in 1880 and was employed by the Bank of New Zealand at Auckland. Before the Native tour he represented Auckland four times in 1886 and 1888 and Hawke's Bay five times in 1887. As the goal-kicker and sometime captain of the Native team, he was the leading points scorer in Britain with 151 in sixty-three matches.

Returning to Australia in 1890, McCausland played twice for New South Wales against Queensland in 1891, became a first-class referee and gained notoriety by sending off William McKenzie of New Zealand ("Off-side Mac") against New South Wales in 1893. McCausland retired as manager of the Newtown branch of the London-Scottish Bank in Sydney.

NEHUA, Wiri (c.1866-1943) Forward and three-quarter.
Selected for the tour while a student at Te Aute College, Nehua was regarded by Eyton as "a strong player and a good kick, but a trifle slow and was not altogether reliable in the back division". He played only eight times in Britain. After the tour, Nehua returned to Whakapara near Whangarei, but nothing is known of his later life.

RENE, Teo (? — ?) Forward.
Rene played for Nelson against New South Wales in 1886 and Wellington in 1887. However, after appearing in six of the nine Native team matches in New Zealand, he injured his foot at Suez on the journey to Britain and did not take the field for a month. He then played forty-three matches in Britain and all of the fixtures back in New Zealand.

Appendix 1: The players

STEWART, David (Heta Reweti) (c.1869-1909) Forward.
One of the most popular, and heaviest, members of the Native team, Stewart appeared at least forty times in Britain. In his later representative rugby career he played two matches for Auckland in 1892 and one in 1893.

A major landowner and racehorse owner at Thames, Stewart was a borough councillor and on the committee of the local jockey club. One of his horses won the Great Northern Derby. He died of Brights disease, leaving a large family.

TAIAROA, Richard (1866-1954) Forward.
Brother of the famed New Zealand player Jack Taiaroa, and a cousin of Tom Ellison, he was born at Otakou on the Otago Peninsula and attended Christchurch Boys High School in its second year, 1882. He made fifty-nine appearances in Britain. In his remaining representative career he played in two matches for Wellington, one each in in 1886 and 1887, and one for Hawke's Bay in 1889.

Apprenticed to a civil engineer in Wellington, Taiaroa then trained as a surveyor and later took control of the family farm at Taumutu, from where he won numerous prizes in Canterbury A&P shows as a cattle breeder. After service in South Africa with the Mounted Rifles during the Boer War, he was a Maori representative at two coronations, those of Edward VII in 1902 and George V in 1910. Awarded the OBE in 1949, he was survived only by Elliot among Native team members.

WARBRICK, Alfred (1860-1940) Forward.
The oldest of the Warbrick brothers, he was also the least able as a rugby player, appearing only four times in Britain and twelve times in Australia and New Zealand. Yet Alf Warbrick's achievements in other areas were considerable. Born near Rotorua, where his father Abraham Warbrick was a Maori interpreter, he was educated in Tauranga and Auckland and then apprenticed as a boatbuilder. Returning to Rotorua, he served as Chief Government Guide for the thermal region for most of the period from 1886 to 1932. During this time he safely conducted more than 10,000 visitors through the area, including ten successive governors or governors-general and the future King George V. Alf Warbrick died at the Knox Home in Auckland.

WARBRICK, Arthur (c.1863-1902) Forward.
Regarded by Eyton as "a most determined tackler ... [who] made the most of his weight and strength", Art Warbrick played forty-six matches in Britain. However, he had no other representative rugby outside the tour. A ferryman at Opotiki, he was drowned in a work accident.

WARBRICK, Frederick (c.1868-1904) Half-back.
The youngest and lightest of the Warbrick brothers, Fred Warbrick improved greatly during the Native tour, playing forty-one matches in Britain and developing a very effective combination with Keogh. Originally employed as a journalist for the *Bay of Plenty Times*, he moved to Australia early in 1890. There he played for the Arfoma club and for Queensland in 1892 and 1893. He also refereed Queensland's match against New Zealand in 1893. As well as working for the Queensland Government Printer, Fred Warbrick owned the Edgewater boarding house at Woody Point, Brisbane, where he died in a boating accident.

WARBRICK, Joseph Astbury (1862-1903) Three-quarter.
Born in Rotorua, Joe Warbrick was a star player in the decade before the Native tour. After education at St Stephen's Native School, he represented Auckland teams in 1877, 1882-83, 1886 and 1894, Wellington in 1879-80, and 1888, and Hawke's Bay in 1885 and 1887. Along with Jack Taiaroa he was one of the first Maori players to represent New Zealand — on the 1884 tour of Australia where he played all seven matches. Sadly, Warbrick's contribution to the Native tour was restricted by injury to only fourteen matches in Britain and seven matches in New Zealand and Australia.

Apparently a government employee after leaving school, Warbrick later farmed near Tauranga. He was a member of the Whakatane County Council and first chairman of the Rangitikei Drainage Board. He was killed in an eruption of the Waimungu geyser near Rotorua.

WARBRICK, William (c.1866- ?) Full-back.
In spite of numerous and severe injuries which restricted his appearances in Britain to only thirty-six matches, Billy Warbrick emerged as one of the outstanding players of the Native team. Eyton described him thus: "a dashing player, grand tackler, first-class kick, very quick at following up, and beyond being occasionally too venturesome, he left nothing to be desired in his play".

His long representative career began with a match for Bay of Plenty Combined Clubs in 1882 and included two appearances for Auckland in 1886 and five more in 1890. Moving to Queensland with his brother, Fred, he represented that colony from 1891 to 1894, including both matches against the 1893 New Zealand team. He also represented New South Wales against the 1897 New Zealand tourists. Although it is commonly believed that Warbrick returned to New Zealand before his death, nothing is known of his life beyond rugby.

WEBSTER, Alexander (Sandy) (c.1869-1893) Forward.
Without any previous representative experience, Webster made an important

Appendix 1: The players

contribution to the first half of the tour of Britain, playing in thirty-five of the first thirty-seven matches. Severely restricted by injury after that, he appeared only three more times. Praised by Eyton for his "quiet and excellent social qualities", he returned to New Zealand before the Australian tour. Employed by a guano company near Dunedin, Webster died in a work accident when his feet were crushed and he was unable to obtain medical assistance.

WILLIAMS, George (Bully) (1856-1925) Forward.
The oldest player in the Native team, and one of its Pakeha members, Williams was born in Auckland, the son of a British army officer. Although he did not play rugby at any level until the age of twenty-four, he soon became a stalwart of the Poneke club, represented Wellington seven times in 1886 and 1887 and Hawke's Bay once in 1887 while stationed in the police force at Hastings. Sometimes captain of the Native team, he played at least fifty-three matches in Britain, but gave up rugby after the tour.

A policeman in Wellington, Hastings and Invercargill, Williams was also a member of the force which arrested the Maori prophet Te Whiti at Parihaka. Retiring to Wellington, his last public appearance was at a reception for the returning "Invincibles" in 1925.

WYNYARD, George (Sherry) (1862- ?) Forward.
The oldest of the three Wynyard brothers in the Native team, Sherry Wynyard had no representative rugby experience other than the tour. He played forty-three matches in Britain and twenty in Australia and New Zealand. Moving to Sydney in the early 1890s, Wynyard played some club football and worked as a builder. He may have returned to New Zealand before 1920.

WYNYARD, Henry (Pie) (c.1865-1921) Half-back.
Not an original selection, but used because he was already in Britain on his own business, Pie Wynyard joined the Native team at Newcastle in November 1888. He played only fourteen matches in Britain and eight in Australia and New Zealand. He completed his representative career with one match for Wellington in 1891 and three in 1892. Employed for many years by the Gear Meat Company at Petone, Pie Wynyard died in Wellington.

WYNYARD, William Thomas (Tabby) (c.1867-1938) Three-quarter.
Born and educated at Devonport, Tabby Wynyard developed as a fine all-round sportsman. He represented both Auckland and Wellington at rugby, cricket and athletics, as well as being an accomplished golfer, oarsman, cyclist and billiards player.

His representative rugby career consisted of matches for Auckland in 1887,

1889, 1895 and 1896, Wellington in 1893 and 1894, and New Zealand on the tour to Australia in 1893. For the Native team he appeared at least fifty-two times in Britain, and off the field achieved great popularity for his singing of "On the Ball". A public servant, Wynyard became district manager of the New Zealand Department of Agriculture in Wellington.

The Management

EYTON, Thomas (c.1843-1925) Promoter.
The son of a lieutenant-commander in the Royal Navy, Eyton was born in Essex, England, and educated at the Royal Naval School, Blackheath. After two years as a clerk at Trinity House, London, he emigrated to New Zealand in 1862.

During the next seven years he served with the Taranaki Bushrangers and Patea Light Horse in the Anglo-Maori wars. After five years based in Wellington as a Treasury employee during the early 1870s, Eyton went into private business as a commission agent at Pihea. In later life he took a considerable interest in the Anglo-Maori War Veterans Association. He died in Auckland.

LAWLOR, Jack (? — ?) Victorian Rules Coach.
In the end, Lawlor's contribution to the Native tour was minimal. Although engaged by Scott as a Victorian Rules coach, he had no opportunity to perform this task amid the hectic British itinerary. According to Eyton he cost the promoters £200 in expenses while performing no useful purpose. Lawlor also added to the injury toll of the tour when he fell from a railway platform at Kirkstall after boarding the wrong train.

A player for the Ballarat and Essendon clubs in Melbourne, and occasionally for the Native team while in Victoria, Lawlor was also engaged as a coach by the touring British team and came to New Zealand to assist them in May 1888.

SCOTT, James (? — c.1894) Manager.
A publican from Gisborne, Scott apparently performed his managerial duties very satisfactorily on tour, in spite of the demanding itinerary. As George Williams put it, "I think I express the opinion of all other members of the team that we might have fared much worse in other hands." Scott died in Nelson shortly before Eyton began writing his account of the tour.

Appendix 2
Match record

Such has been the obscurity of the Native team, that even its itinerary is a matter for some debate. The main problem arises with the Australian section of the tour where matches were played under Victorian and Association rules as well as rugby. Eyton, in *Rugby Football Past and Present,* records that in total the team played 108 matches, won eighty, drew five and lost twenty-three. In his book, Tom Ellison claims only 69 wins from 108 matches. Neither provides a full itinerary to support their figures.

The version commonly accepted now, and used here, is that of Arthur Swan: 107 matches played, seventy-eight wins, six draws and twenty-three losses. The number of discrepancies with Eyton suggest that Swan obtained his information from another source, perhaps from an account kept by Scott. However, its accuracy can be taken from team lists and individual scoring records, which support all but a few matches.

IN BRITISH ISLES
1888

Oct. 3–v. Surrey	At Richmond	Won 4 to 1
Oct. 6–v. Northamptonshire	At Northampton	Won 12 to 0
Oct.10–v. Kent	At Blackheath	Won 4 to 1
Oct.13–v. Moseley	At Moseley	Lost 4 to 6
Oct.18–v. Burton-on-Trent	At Burton-on-Trent	Lost 3 to 4
Oct.20–v. Midland Counties	At Birmingham	Won 10 to 0
Oct.22–v. Middlesex	At Fletching	Lost 0 to 9
Oct.24–v. Hull	At Hull	Lost 0 to 1
Oct.27–v. Dewsbury	At Dewsbury	Won 6 to 0
Oct.31–v. Wakefield Trinity	At Wakefield	Lost 0 to 1
Nov. 3–v. Northumberland County	At Newcastle	Drew 3 to 3
Nov. 5–v. Stockton-on-Tees	At Stockton	Won 6 to 1
Nov. 7–v. Tynemouth	At North Shields	Won 7 to 1
Nov.10–v. Halifax Free Wanderers	At Halifax	Lost 4 to 13
Nov.12–v. Newcastle and District	At Newcastle	Won 14 to 0
Nov.14–v. Hartlepool Rovers	At Hartlepool	Won 1 to 0
Nov.17–v. Cumberland County	At Maryport	Won 10 to 2
Nov.20–v. Carlisle	At Carlisle	Won 13 to 0
Nov.22–v. Hawick	At Hawick	Won 3 to 1
Nov.23–v. East Cumberland	At Carlisle	Won 12 to 0
Nov.24–v. Westmorland County	At Kendal	Won 3 to 1
Nov.26–v. Swinton	At Swinton	Lost 0 to 2

Forerunners of the All Blacks

Nov.28-v. Liverpool and District	At Liverpool	Won 9 to 0
Dec. 1-v. IRELAND	At Dublin	Won 13 to 4
Dec. 3-v. Trinity College	At Dublin	Drew 4 to 4
Dec. 5-v. North of Ireland	At Belfast	Won 2 to 0
Dec. 8-v. Lancashire County	At Manchester	Lost 0 to 1
Dec.10-v. Batley	At Batley	Drew 5 to 5
Dec.12-v. Yorkshire County	At Manningham	Won 10 to 6
Dec.15-v. Broughton Rangers	At Broughton	Won 8 to 0
Dec.17-v. Wigan	At Wigan	Won 5 to 1
Dec.19-v. Llanelli	At Llanelli	Lost 0 to 3
Dec.22-v. WALES	At Swansea	Lost 0 to 5
Dec.24-v. Swansea	At Swansea	Won 5 to 0
Dec.26-v. Newport	At Newport	Won 3 to 0
Dec.29-v. Cardiff	At Cardiff	Lost 1 to 4
Jan. 1-v. Bradford	At Bradford	Lost 1 to 4
Jan. 3-v. Leeds Parish Church	At Leeds	Won 6 to 3
Jan. 5-v. Kirkstall	At Kirkstall	Won 7 to 3
Jan. 7-v. Brighouse Rangers	At Brighouse	Won 4 to 0
Jan. 9-v. Huddersfield	At Huddersfield	Won 7 to 6
Jan. 12-v. Stockport	At Stockport	Drew 3 to 3
Jan. 14-v. Castleford	At Castleford	Lost 3 to 9
Jan. 17-v. Warrington	At Warrington	Won 7 to 1
Jan. 19-v. Yorkshire County	At Wakefield	Lost 4 to 16
Jan. 23-v. Spen Valley District	At Cleckheaton	Won 8 to 7
Jan. 26-v. Somersetshire County	At Wellington	Won 17 to 4
Jan. 30-v. Devonshire County	At Exeter	Won 12 to 0
Jan. 31-v. Taunton	At Taunton	Won 8 to 0
Feb. 2-v. Gloucestershire County	At Gloucester	Won 4 to 1
Feb. 4-v. Midland Counties	At Moseley	Won 6 to 1
Feb. 6-v. Blackheath Rovers	At Blackheath	Won 9 to 3
Feb. 9-v. United Services	At Portsmouth	Won 10 to 0
Feb. 16-v. ENGLAND	At Blackheath	Lost 0 to 7
Feb. 18-v. London Welsh	At Richmond	Won 2 to 1
Feb. 19-v. Cambridge University	At Cambridge	Lost 3 to 7
Feb. 21-v. Oxford University	At Oxford	Lost 0 to 6
Feb. 23-v Manningham	At Manningham	Won 4 to 0
Feb. 25-v. St John's, Leeds	At Leeds	Won 9 to 0
Feb. 27-v. Leigh	At Leigh	Lost 1 to 4
Mar. 2-v. Runcorn	At Runcorn	Won 8 to 3
Mar. 4-v. Oldham	At Oldham	Lost 0 to 6
Mar. 5-v. Halifax Free Wanderers	At Halifax	Won 6 to 0
Mar. 7-v. Barrow and District	At Barrow	Lost 0 to 3
Mar. 9-v. Widnes	At Widnes	Won 8 to 1
Mar. 11-v. Manchester	At Manchester	Won 7 to 1
Mar. 13-v. Walkden	At Walkden	Won 6 to 1
Mar. 14-v. St Helens	At St Helens	Won 9 to 0
Mar. 16-v. Salford	At Salford	Won 7 to 1
Mar. 18-v. Rochdale Hornets	At Rochdale	Won 10 to 0
Mar. 20-v. York	At York	Won 4 to 3
Mar. 23-v. Hull	At Hull	Drew 1 to 1
Mar. 25-v. Widnes	At Widnes	Won 6 to 1
Mar. 27-v. Southern Counties	At Leyton	Won 3 to 1

Played 74: Won 49: Drawn 5: Lost 20.
Points for, 394: Points against, 188.

Appendix 2: Match record

IN AUSTRALIA
1888
1889

Aug.11-v. Melbourne	At Melbourne	Won 3 to 0
Aug.15-v. Melbourne	At Melbourne	Drew 1 to 1

1889

May 24-v. Melbourne	At Melbourne	Won 13 to 6
May 31-v. Navy Team XVIII	At Melbourne	Won 13 to 6
June 11-v. Victoria	At Melbourne	Won 19 to 0
June 15-v. New South Wales	At Sydney	Won 12 to 9
June 17-v. Uni. of Sydney	At Sydney	Won 17 to 7
June 19-v. Parramatta Club and King's School XVIII	At Sydney	Won 21 to 0
June 22-v. New South Wales	At Sydney	Won 16 to 12
June 25-v. Arfoma	At Sydney	Won 27 to 3
June 28-v. Permanent Artillery XVIII	At Sydney	Won 32 to 10
July 15-v. Queensland	At Brisbane	Won 22 to 0
July 17-v. Toowoomba XVI	At Toowoomba	Won 16 to 0
July 19-v. Ipswich	At Ipswich	Won 17 to 5
July 22-v. Queensland	At Brisbane	Won 11 to 7
July 24-v. Toowoomba XVII	At Toowoomba	Won 19 to 0

Played 16: Won 15: Drawn 1: Lost 0.
Points for, 239: Points against, 66.

IN NEW ZEALAND
1888
1889

June 23-v. Hawke's Bay	At Napier	Won 5 to 0
June 30-v. Hawke's Bay	At Napier	Won 11 to 0
July 7-v. Auckland	At Auckland	Lost 0 to 9
July 11-v. Nelson	At Nelson	Won 9 to 0
July 14-v. Wellington	At Wellington	Won 3 to 0
July 21-v. Canterbury	At Christchurch	Won 5 to 4
July 24-v. South Canterbury	At Timaru	Won 9 to 0
July 28-v. Otago	At Dunedin	Lost 0 to 8
July 31-v. Otago	At Dunedin	Won 1 to 0

1889

Aug. 7-v. Southland	At Invercargill	Won 5 to 1
Aug. 8-v. Mataura Dist. XVI	At Gore	Won 16 to 3
Aug.10-v. Otago	At Dunedin	Won 11 to 8
Aug.15-v. Hawke's Bay	At Christchurch	Won 13 to 2
Aug.17-v. Canterbury	At Christchurch	Won 15 to 0
Aug.19-v. Wairarapa	At Masterton	Won 10 to 8
Aug.20-v. Wellington	At Wellington	Won 4 to 1
Aug.24-v. Auckland	At Auckland	Lost 2 to 7

Played 17: Won 14: Drawn 0: Lost 3.
Points for, 119: Points against, 51.

Grand Totals: Played 107: Won 78: Drawn 6: Lost 23.
Points for, 772: Points against, 305.

Forerunners of the All Blacks

VICTORIAN RULES MATCHES

The following is a record of those matches which can be traced in the Melbourne press. The frequency of matches in relation to those played under rugby rules, suggests that it is complete, because the team left Melbourne after the rugby match against Victoria on 10 June.

May 15–v. Maryborough	At Maryborough	Lost 1/2 to 6/9
May 18–v. Ballarat	At Ballarat	Lost 0/4 to 4/2
May 25–v. Carlton	At Melbourne	Lost 2/4 to 13/16
May 28–v. Wanderers	At Melbourne	Won 10/11 to 2/3
May 30–v. South Melbourne	At Melbourne	Won 6/4 to 4/13
June 1–v. St Kilda	At Melbourne	Lost 1/6 to 6/7
June 6–v. Daylesford	At Daylesford	Won 2/4 to 1/5
June 8–v. Essendon	At Melbourne	Lost 5/5 to 11/14

Played 8: Won 3: Drawn 0: Lost 5.

Appendix 3
Individual records

APPEARANCES

In many cases the figures provided here indicate only a minimum number of appearances. The team lists for six matches in Britain and five in Australia are either incomplete or non-existent. In Britain the six opponents were: East Cumberland; Brighouse Rangers; Taunton; Leigh; Barrow and District; St Helens. The five Australian teams for which lists are missing are: Navy XVIII; Victoria; Parramatta and King's School XVIII; Arfoma; Permanent Artillery XVIII.

	Britain	Australia	New Zealand	Total
W. Elliot	63	10	13	86
R.G. Taiaroa	59	9	17	85
T.R. Ellison	58	9	16	83
D.R. Gage	68	1	13	82
G.A. Williams	53	8	14	75
W.T. Wynyard	52	8	15	75
P. Keogh	60	9	1	70
Art Warbrick.	46	8	13	67
E. McCausland	63	1	2	66
F. Warbrick	41	10	14	65
G. Wynyard	43	9	11	63
H. Lee	50	7	5	62
W. Warbrick	36	6	17	59
W. Anderson	48	5	5	58
T. Rene	34	7	14	55
R. Maynard	38	7	9	54
D. Stewart	40	4	8	52
W. Karauria	43	2	5	50
C. Madigan	32	8	10	50
A. Webster	37	1	7	45
C. Goldsmith	20	5	10	35
E. Ihimaira	14	2	7	23
H. Wynyard	14	2	6	22
J. Warbrick	14	2	5	21
W. Nehua	8	3	7	18
Alf Warbrick	4	4	8	16

SCORING
IN BRITISH ISLES

	T	C	PG	M	DG	Tl
E. McCausland	2	64	3	2	2	151
W.T. Wynyard	23	-	-	-	7	44
T.R. Ellison	23	6	1	-	-	38
P. Keogh	34	-	-	-	-	34
W. Elliot	21	-	-	-	-	21
G.A. Williams	12	4	-	-	-	20
D.R. Gage	13	-	-	-	2	19
E. Ihimaira	8	-	-	-	-	8
C. Madigan	7	-	-	-	-	7
F. Warbrick	5	1	-	-	-	7
W. Karauria	6	-	-	-	-	6
H. Lee	6	-	-	-	-	6
Arthur Warbrick	5	-	-	-	-	5
W. Warbrick	5	-	-	-	-	5
D. Stewart	5	-	-	-	-	5
G. Wynyard	4	-	-	-	-	4
R.G. Taiaroa	3	-	-	-	-	3
R. Maynard	2	-	-	-	-	2
H.J. Wynyard	2	-	-	-	-	2
J.A. Warbrick	-	1	-	-	-	2
T. Rene	1	-	-	-	-	1
W. Nehua	1	-	-	-	-	1
C. Goldsmith	1	-	-	-	-	1
W. Anderson	1	-	-	-	-	1
A. Webster	1	-	-	-	-	1
Total.	191	76	4	2	11	394

IN AUSTRALIA
Victoria

	T	C	PG	M	DG	Tl
F. Warbrick	3★	2	-	-	-	9
W.T. Wynyard	1★	2	-	-	-	7
P. Keogh	4★	-	-	-	-	6
H. Lee	1	2	-	-	-	5
R. Maynard	1★	1	-	-	-	5
C Madigan	4	-	-	-	-	4
G.A. Williams	1★	-	-	-	-	3
T.R. Ellison	1★	-	-	-	-	3
E. McCausland	-	1	-	-	-	2
Arthur Warbrick	1	-	-	-	-	1
E. Ihimaira	1	-	-	-	-	1
W. Nehua	1	-	-	-	-	1
W. Anderson	1	-	-	-	-	1
C. Goldsmith	1	-	-	-	-	1
Total.	21	9	-	-	-	49

★ Includes one try which counted three points.

Appendix 3: Individual records

New South Wales

	T	C	PG	M	DG	Tl
T.R. Ellison	4	1	-	-	-	14
R. Maynard	2	4	-	-	-	14
C. Madigan	4	-	-	-	-	12
G.A. Williams	1	4	-	-	-	11
W.T. Wynyard	3	-	-	-	-	9
W. Warbrick	3	-	-	-	-	9
F. Warbrick	3	-	-	-	-	9
C. Goldsmith	3	-	-	-	-	9
G. Wynyard	2	-	-	-	-	6
H. Lee	2	-	-	-	-	6
P. Keogh	2	-	-	-	-	6
H. Wynyard	1	-	-	-	-	3
R.G. Taiaroa	1	-	-	-	-	3
W. Nehua	1	-	-	-	-	3
D. Stewart	1	-	-	-	-	3
E. McCausland	-	1	-	-	-	2
Total	35	10	-	-	-	125

Queensland

	T	C	PG	M	DG	Tl
T.R. Ellison	5	5	-	-	-	25
F. Warbrick	2	2	-	-	-	10
P. Keogh	4	-	-	-	-	8
W.T. Wynyard	2	-	-	-	1	8
W. Elliot	3	-	-	-	-	6
R. Maynard	1	1	-	-	-	5
C. Madigan	2	-	-	-	-	4
H. Lee	2	-	-	-	-	4
W. Nehua	-	1	-	-	-	3
H.C. Speakman*	1	-	-	-	-	2
C. Goldsmith	1	-	-	-	-	2
Art. Warbrick	1	-	-	-	-	2
Alf Warbrick	1	-	-	-	-	2
G.A. Williams	1	-	-	-	-	2.
W. Warbrick	1	-	-	-	-	2
Total	27	9	-	-	1	85

*Speakman, a member of the 1888 British team who settled in Queensland, played in the second Toowoomba match.

NEW ZEALAND

	T	C	PG	M	DG	Tl
T.R. Ellison	10	10	-	1	-	33
W.T. Wynyard	7	1	-	1	1	15
D.R. Gage	5	-	-	-	2	11
W. Elliot	10	-	-	-	-	10
F. Warbrick	5	2	-	-	-	9
J. Warbrick	1	2	-	1	-	8
C Goldsmith	4	-	-	-	-	4
E. Ihimaira	4	-	-	-	-	4
W. Nehua	-	2	-	-	-	4
R.G. Taiaroa	4	-	-	-	-	4
W. Warbrick	4	-	-	-	-	4
G.A. Williams	2	1	-	-	-	4
Alf Warbrick	3	-	-	-	-	3
R. Maynard	2	-	-	-	-	2
P. Keogh	1	-	-	-	-	1
C. Madigan	1	-	-	-	-	1
T. Rene	1	-	-	-	-	1
H. Wynyard	1	-	-	-	-	1
Total	65	18	-	3	3	119

In New Zealand, the British Isles and Victoria, tries counted one point; conversions two points; all other goals three points.

In New South Wales tries counted three points; conversions two points; dropped goals four points.

In Queensland tries counted two points; conversions three points; dropped goals four points.

Bibliographical note

The single greatest obstacle to understanding the Native team is a lack of reliable primary sources — especially accounts by the players. Although Eyton suggests that a number of diaries were kept during the tour, only that by Wiri Nehua has survived. Written in Maori, and currently being translated at La Trobe University, Melbourne, it has been described as little more than a chronological "trip book". It was not available to the author. Tom Ellison provides a few rather anecdotal paragraphs on the tour in his book *The Art of Rugby Football*, and there are short comments by Joe Warbrick, George Williams and Pie Wynyard in Eyton's *Rugby Football Past and Present*.

As all of Joe Warbrick's personal papers were destroyed in a fire in 1893, the task of writing an account of the tour fell to Eyton — who did so in response to numerous enquiries. Judging by certain inclusions that are less than favourable to the team, such as the Middlesex incident and the Brisbane affair, this is an honest and revealing summary of the tour. It does not, however, reinforce many of its main points with substantial detail, and is particularly sparse in its coverage of the crucial periods of the tour in New Zealand.

The most productive sources of information on the Native team are the various New Zealand, Australian and British newspapers. The British sporting press gave regular coverage to the team both on and off the field — albeit on a regional basis; *The Field* of London did not give coverage to matches in the north, in the same manner that the *Athletic News* of Manchester ignored all but the England international among southern matches. Numerous provincial and local papers gave lengthy accounts of individual matches in the north and west of England. Among the New Zealand press, only the *Lyttelton Times* seems to have had access to a correspondent in fairly regular contact with the team. Most simply relied on reprints of existing British reports which were shipped to New Zealand and published roughly seven weeks after events had occurred.

A number of secondary sources proved particularly useful. A.C. Swan's monumental *History of New Zealand Rugby Football 1870-1945*, (Wellington 1948) and R.H. Chester and N.A.C. McMillan *The Encyclopedia of New Zealand Rugby*, (Auckland 1981) and *The Visitors*, (Auckland 1990) were valuable for statistical details of the tour and biographical details of some players. For the context in which the Native team played, three books were essential in explaining the relationship between sport and society in nineteenth century Britain: E. Dunning and K. Sheard, *Barbarians, Gentlemen and Players: A Sociological Study of the Development of Rugby Football,* (Canberra 1979); R. Holt, *Sport and the British,* (Oxford 1989); T. Mason, ed., *Sport in Britain: A Social History,* (Cambridge 1989). Elements of the New Zealand context are examined by J.O.C. Phillips, *A Man's Country?,* (Auckland 1987). R. Gate, *Rugby League: An Illustrated History,* (London 1989) gives a perceptive account of north/south tensions in English rugby during the 1880s.

A complete bibliography, including more than seventy newspapers with material relating to the Native team, is contained in my MA thesis.

Index

Aboriginal cricket team 18-19, 22, 53, 103-4
amateurism 36, 87-8
alcohol 47, 96, 103, 116
All Blacks (1905, 1924) 11, 119-23
Anderson, W. 26-7, 108, 133
Auckland match — proposed v. British team, 14f.
Auckland — v. Native Team, 32-3, 116-17
Auckland Rugby Football Union 118

Brisbane affair 111-3, 125
British rugby: standard of, 57, 106; limits on popularity of, 62f; northern approach to, 91f.
British team (1888) 13, 19, 36, 87, 94.
Brown, — (Mr), 19, 37

Canterbury — v. Native Team, 41, 115-6, 117-8
Canterbury Rugby Football Union 37
Carlisle — v. Native Team 58-9
champagne incident 47-8, 104, 125
colonial expectations 33-4, 42, 105

Elliot, William ("Mother") 28, 104, 127, 133.
Ellison, Thomas R. 23-5, 83-5, 93, 100, 106, 127, 133-4
England international 11-12, 83-6, 93, 125
Evershed, Frank 83
Eyton, Thomas 14-15, 38, 40, 69, 100, 102, 104, 123, 140

finances 18, 19-21, 31, 62f, 108

gambling 29, 34, 103, 111, 112-3
Gage, David R. 25, 107, 127, 134

Goldsmith, Charles (Taare Koropiti) 26, 111, 134

haka 52-3
Hawick — v. Native Team 59-60
Hawke's Bay — v. Native Team, 32, 114-5, 117
Hawke's Bay Rugby Football Union 30, 39-40, 117
Hill, George Rowland 11, 46, 47, 83-5, 87, 91-2
Hilton, — (Mr) 103

Ihimaira, E. (Smiler) 26, 107-8, 134-5
injuries 44, 46, 58, 67-8, 69, 70-1, 82, 95, 99, 126
Ireland international 71-5

Karauria, Wi 25-6, 99, 108, 135
Keogh, Patrick 28-9, 69, 111, 113, 114, 126, 127, 135

Lawlor, Jack 43, 108, 140
Lee, Harry 25, 135
Lyttelton Times correspondent 68, 94-5, 99

Madigan, Charles 28, 60, 69, 81, 111, 113, 136
Marshall, Rev. Frank 38, 52
Maynard, Richard (Dick), 25, 136
McCausland, Edward E.M. (Mac) 28, 85, 108, 136
Middlesex — v. Native Team 47-9

Native team. *See* New Zealand Native Football Representatives.
Nehua, Wiri 26, 136
NZ Native Football Representatives (Native Team): conduct (off-field), 34,

103-5; goal-kicking record, 41, 110; name change, 29; organization of, 13f, 30; selection policy, 23f, 27, 66; size of, 29-30; strength of, 31-2, 33, 46, 78-9, 121-2; tensions within, 68-70, 107.
New Zealand Rugby Football Union 93, 103, 119
Northern Union (Rugby League) 92, 120-2
Northern Rugby Union (Queensland) 111

Otago — v. Native Team 41-2, 114
Otago Rugby Football Union 39, 111-2, 113, 117, 119

Pakeha player controversy 27-8, 39-40
public schools 15, 51, 57, 87-8, 92-3
professionalism 34-9, 92, 113, 119

Queensland — v. Native Team, 110-11

racial attitudes 18, 19-20, 23, 44-5, 51-5, 71, 100
Rene, Teo 25, 44, 136
rough play 42, 89-90, 91-2, 94-5
rugby: origins, 15-16; established in New Zealand, 17, 92-3; Maori, 17, 18
Rugby Football Union (England) 11-12, 14, 36, 64, 82-3, 85, 91-2, 93-4, 99, 100, 120

Scott, James R. 15, 40, 43, 57, 62-4, 66, 69, 100, 102, 123, 140
Shrewsbury, Arthur 37-8, 61
Soccer 62, 110

Somersetshire — v. Native Team, 81
Southern Counties — v. Native Team 99
Speakman, Charles 111
speculation 60-61
sporting imperialism 33, 49-51, 87-8
sportsmanship: criticism of Native team 42, 87f, 100, 117-8; praise, 90-91, 94
Stewart, David 27, 108, 137
Stoddart, Andrew 11, 83
Surrey — v. Native Team, 45-6

Taiaroa, Jack 14, 23, 41
Taiaroa, Richard (Dick) 23, 59-60, 137
Te Aute College 17, 26
"Threequarter-back" 33, 37.42

Victorian (Australian) Rules 43, 108-09

Wales international 76-8
Warbrick, Alfred 23, 69, 137
Warbrick, Arthur 23, 111, 137
Warbrick, Frederick 23, 138
Warbrick, Joseph 12-13, 17, 21, 33, 37, 58, 69, 80-81, 94, 103, 105, 121, 138
Warbrick, William (Billy) 23, 111, 138
Webster, Alexander (Sandy) 26-7, 108, 138-9
Wellington Rugby Football Union 118
Williams, George (Bully) 28, 39, 121, 127, 139
Wynyard, George (Sherry) 25, 139
Wynyard, Henry (Pie) 25, 70, 75, 105, 139
Wynyard, William T. (Tabby) 25, 126, 139-40

Yorkshire — v. Native Team 75-6, 81